I am the Border, so I am

I am the Border, so I am

@BorderIrish

HarperCollins*Publishers*

HarperCollins*Publishers*
1 London Bridge Street
London SE1 9GF

www.harpercollins.co.uk

First published by HarperCollins*Publishers* 2019

5 7 9 10 8 6 4

© @BorderIrish 2019

asserts the moral right to be

road 96, 209,
225, (p45);

pin);
(p211);

'Lik of Hell',

ISBN 978-0-00-835699-6

Printed and bound in Great Britain by
CPI Group (UK) Ltd, Croydon

MIX
Paper from
responsible sources
FSC™ C007454

This book is produced from independently certified FSC™ paper
to ensure responsible forest management.

For more information visit: www.harpercollins.co.uk/green

Howareye?

Well, now. How's it going? C'mere to me, I was just minding my own business, being a largely invisible border that no one had thought about for years. And happy enough I was with that. It's a tiring business, bordering. It's a generally unhappy one too, at the best of times. But after decades of misery, there was me, semi-retired, a bit sleepy, carefree as a border can be. And then along comes Brexit.

BREXIT.

The very word makes me a bit green.

It caught me by surprise when it happened. You're probably the same yourself. I woke up one morning and shook my grass, looking forward to another day of doing not very much, and there was a whole load of paparazzi, with the cameras flashing, shouting, 'Hey, Irish Border! Look dark! Look threatening! Look sexy!'

Well, now, I'm attractive enough to look at, for a border, but it's long since I appeared threatening to man or beast. I pulled the grass back around myself and tried to ignore them. They're persistent, though, these fellas with the cameras, and they caught me a bit off-guard. So those early Brexit photos don't show my best side. Then the journalists started to turn up, with all their daft questions: 'How did you get here? Are you scared? How do you *really* feel?' Hiding from British journalists sent by their editors to find me has been the only fun thing about Brexit. They write articles saying they've 'straddled' me (I know, the cheek of them) because they love to sound macho, but that actually means they couldn't find me. So they guess I was somewhere in between all the windblown sheughs and the fields they got lost in before they wrote their article about me, holed up in a floral-curtained, swirly-carpeted Newry B&B while eating a saturated-fat local breakfast special.

Yes, I had thought I was going to go into retirement. I'd imagined a nice little EU-funded Museum of Myself in a few decades' time, with a coffee shop and border-themed ice cream, but oh no. Along came Brexit, like some gobshite taking its first driving lesson, crashing all over the place. I took one look at Brexit and, says I to myself, 'If a stop isn't put to this soon I'll be back to proper full-on bordering again. And I am a bit old for that kind of thing.'

'How old are you, Border?' I hear you saying, fictional reader. Well, now, there's a question. It's very hard to say. Do you ever think to yourself, 'I'll do this wee job as a stopgap, just to keep things ticking over until my creative career really takes off, and then 97-odd years later you look at yourself and you're still doing the same thing?' That's me. I was meant to move after a few years, but you know what humans are like. Indecisive. Time passes fair quick, doesn't it? But also very slowly, says you. And that's the truth as well. But time has passed, and thank the Lord above for it, because time has had little enough useful to offer me this past century except the last twenty-odd years since the Good Friday Agreement. They've been grand, in comparison, those two decades of birdsong. But, in hindsight, now that I put my mind to it, and ponder recent events, maybe I was a bit too reclusive since 1998. Maybe I was a complacent border.

You know that way you put something down in a place and then that's the place the thing stays? And then, you know that thing when something is really important and you put it somewhere obvious so you'll remember it? And then you forget about it? And then later (let's say, over 97 years later) you fall over it in the middle of the night? Yeah? That's the British government and me. Completely forgot about me. Eejits.

Back in the 1920s, a panel of 'experts' of different political persuasions were meant to re-draw me one day on a tea break. But they argued with each other, as official people do, and nothing changed. It wasn't the first time, and by God it wasn't the last time, that men in suits argued about where I should be, what I should do and how to cross me. I think this is why I'm so at home on Twitter; it's full of people pretending they know what they're doing but never getting anywhere.

When Brexit finally had my nerves completely wrecked, my friend Jean says to me, 'Border, ah come on now, you're going to have to speak up for yourself.'

Jean and I have known each other forever and she's always worth listening to. Maybe not always. She's generally worth listening to.

'Jean,' I said, 'I'm a geopolitical line of demarcation between two countries in the EU. I'm also politically contentious, a bit pointless and totally covered in grass, ruminants of various shapes and sizes, roads of a major and minor kind, and I have a penchant for talking in overly long sentences when I get going. How the hell am I going to get myself heard?'

'Twitter!' Jean said. 'It's perfect for spouting about politics when you're not really sure what's going on.'

'Grand,' says I, 'I'll give it a lash.'

So this is me, @BorderIrish. I used @BorderIrish because Jean said it sounded cool and interesting, and @TheBorderImposedbytheBritishonIrelandAgainsttheWilloftheMajorityofthePeopleoftheIslandThoughNotAlltobeTotallyFairAboutIt is too long for a Twitter handle, apparently. Though it has never stopped anyone on Twitter suggesting I use it.

8

Jean told me I was made for Twitter. She'd read in a history book that when Michael Collins went in to Downing Street in 1921 to negotiate the Treaty, he said to Lloyd George, 'The Irish are a sovereign people. We cannot accept the partition of the island.'

And Lloyd George replied, 'Mr Collins, consider the metaphysical Twitter possibilities we would put in place for future generations.' Big Mick hadn't thought of this. Ten minutes later they were shaking hands and Collins had agreed to take the 26 counties while the sovereign people waited for someone to invent Twitter. Apparently de Valera sent Collins to do the negotiating because he knew it would end up in a stupid Twitter account and he didn't want the blame for it. Then there was a civil war. Jean's some reader, always with the book in her hand, so I'm sure this is all true.

That's how I ended up on Twitter in the middle of this Brexit ruination. It's how I've made myself heard and how, in my own small and insignificant way, I have totally messed up Brexit.

I have been pursuing the ironic strategy of having to shout to stay quiet, to be seen to be invisible, to be surreal in order to continue with my mundane reality.

This is how preposterous Brexit has made me. It's very tiring – but oh, sometimes it's worth it for the craic. Do you ever have the feeling that you're talking absolute sh*te but the sh*te you're talking is less sh*te than most of the other sh*te being talked, and *way* less sh*te than the worst sh*te being talked, so you might as well head on with yer own sh*tetalking? That's Twitter.

Still, it's important. I am a mere border. I have no brain, no feet, and definitely no robot lawn-mower like David Davis does, but I care about all my peoples on either side of me. And I do not completely believe anymore that the UK government does. I just want to be a subliminally existing and unobtrusive border giving vague definition to increasingly mean- ingless and nostalgically pointless political ideologies which no one can quite remember other than as a commodified feature of tourist kitsch. I am a GPS-con- fusing, soft-as-the-bee's-wing-brushing-on-lily-petal, jingoism-defying, Brexit-blocking, human-loving, peace-miracle-working, physical-infrastructureless, data-roaming-contradicting, wryly-amusing, caught- in-a-very-bad-situation-comedy kind of border.

I have no idea what's going to happen to me.
Maybe there'll be No Deal. I lie awake at night,
thinking about No Deal. I look at the stars above,
and remember the customs posts, and the men in
uniforms, and the women with the butter hidden
in places I wouldn't look at. And then I remember
the checkpoints and the soldiers. And the pain.
The pain and the mourning. Every day. You
have to stand up to people who disrespect you,
who make promises and then break them, who
think their agenda is more important than

yours, who say they're listening but are actually
thinking about themselves while staring at you.
You have to stand up for yourself.

So I am standing up for myself, online and in print. I'm a line, though not materially so, and that's a little hard to figure. Think of me as grass shimmering gently in a heat haze and that will give an approximate sense of how overwhelmingly attractive I am. Think of my mind as being like an Irish *Last of the Summer Wine* but about Brexit and with a twist of Kierkegaard. Think of me as *The Times* crossword – solved daily, and yet next morning you open the paper and there I am again with no answers filled in.

Think of me as something you can forget, though,
and I'll let you know you picked the wrong
border to forget about.

I'm a functioning, actually-existing constructive ambiguity, an accommodation of irreconcilabilities. A post-borderist border who is staying post-borderist, thank you very much. That annoys people who want firm lines and certainty and absolutes and things that are singularly simplesimplesimple, but I can't be that. I won't.

If you read this here book, or follow me on Twitter, you'll know I joke about it, but Brexit is serious – lives and limbs and loves and losses, mornings and mournings and moorings and migrations, jobs and lazy afternoons and evening kisses and lie-ins and tall tales – they could all change because of Brexit. If I could sing it'd be sweeter than the nightingale's song, but I can't. Still and all, here I am, so I am, and heard I will be.

Twitter Archive

Bord26489713

@BorderStudent

I did it! Graduated today from Bordering School!
Stoked to be starting out on my bordering career in
this febrile post-war world!

3:51 pm – 5 July 1919

The Temporary Irish Border

@BorderIrish

Some personal news – just got new job as
temporary Irish border. Excited to get bordering for
real on the beautiful 'Emerald Isle'!

9:42 am – 3 May 1921

The Temporary Irish Border

@BorderIrish

Humbled to have become a (temporary!)
international border. Wow! Look at me, Mum!

10:11 am – 7 December 1922

The Irish Border
@BorderIrish

I'm going to be stuck in this deadend job forever, amn't I? Boundary Commission my arse

11:26 am – 20 December 1925

The Irish Border
@BorderIrish

New Year's Day. Well woo-f***ing-hoo here I am still on this miserable, rain-sodden island with no one to talk to other than Flann O'Brien and 2 ducks

11:02 am – 1 January 1939

Bernie McFadden & Co
Solicitors, so we are

Newry and Border Area Branch

14.2.18

Hello Border,

I hope you don't mind me getting on to you and maybe we could forget that time with the stolen geese. I was only follwoing my client's instructions. Here, I was thinking, this Brexit's some piece of work and you might be needing a solicitor with a good constitutional background. I also have access to a bit of dirt on the some of the Brexity lads. What do you think? Pro bono, like.

Cheers now,

Bernie

There's an ancient saying around here: 'When the blossom is on the whitethorn, when the swallows return, your cack-handed attempt at re-animating the corpse of Reaganomics via rancid populism will founder on the rock of human goodness.'

Brexit Is Like . . .

It's like the way this afternoon, there I was watching a guy in Pettigo trying to build a garden shed. He had it half built. Then it fell down. His neighbour looked over the fence and said, 'Sam, are you ok?' Sam said, 'I've made a complete f***ing Brexit of it.' And his neighbour said, 'You have, surely.'

It's like the way you say, 'Regulatory divergence may mean some border checks' but I hear 'We're going to make you wear flares and listen to prog rock and generally make like it's the early 70s'.

It's like the way you drift off to sleep and then suddenly wake up and kick the bedclothes off, as if someone's attacking you, and then your heart races for a while and you're all alert and can't get back to sleep. That's what being a hard border is like, over and over again.

It's like when people say, 'There must be an innovative technological solution to the Irish Border problem' and I say, 'Aye, there is. Get a specially designed centralised government computer system and type in the word BREXIT, so that everyone can see it. Then you press DELETE 6 times. Then RETURN.'

It's like when Jim's mum knitted him a jumper in purple with big long sleeves and she didn't get the neckline quite right and he went out wearing it and the other kids laughed at him and his mum said they're just jealous, Jim, but Jim wasn't quite sure if that was true.

I'm like *The Times* simple crossword puzzle: easily solved every day by people who can't be bothered trying the cryptic one.

It's like that thing when you're doing your job perfectly well and then along come some daft management consultants who know nothing about what you do and they make a complete mess of it.

Me (left)
Brexit (right)

Jim!

'Jim!' I blurted out. I couldn't help it.

'Yes, Border.'

'What are you doing, Jim?'

'Just standing here.'

'I see that, Jim. There's no disputing the fact that you're standing there, and fair play to you, Jim, you're excellent at it. And I don't mind you standing there. You're as well there as anywhere, and probably better. There's worse places you could be standing than beside me, Jim. Nevertheless, and I hope you won't begrudge me raising this with you, but I recall now that you said you were Leaving ...'

'I am.'

'And similarly, and correct me if I'm wrong, Jim, I recall that you said this three years ago. In the year of our Lord two thousand and sixteen to be precise.'

'That's right.'

'Years ago now. And yet, one might say, without intended criticism of your lack of activity on the Leaving front, you've been standing there since then.'

'And doing nothing, Border.'

'Doing, as you say yourself, Jim, nothing.'

'I'm Leaving, Border.'

'Ok, Jim.'

Now, look, you know me by now. I'm not going to stop anybody Leaving. Nor, within reason, am I going to stop anybody standing still doing zilch. It just struck me that there was something of a gap between Jim's belief that he was going somewhere and the fact that he wasn't. Clearly Jim is, in his own mind, a Leaver, but his Leaving skills seemed a bit underdeveloped. It's interesting, in a mind-numbingly paralysing way, to think about this Brexity paradox.

It crossed my mind that maybe he needed a little help, or at least that it might help him to talk about it. The UK negotiators kept using the phrase 'reach out'. They'd say things like, 'I'm going to reach out to the Irish side,' which I thought was weird and probably illegal the first time I heard it, but eventually I realised they just meant 'talk to without shouting at'. So I reached out to Jim, idiomatically.

'Jim.'

'Yes, Border.'

'Have you thought about how to Leave?'

'In what way?'

'Moving is not really my area of expertise, Jim, but just off the top of my head, you could go that way, or that way. You could walk or run or even take a plane.'

'You're being difficult now. I'm Leaving.'

'Ok, Jim.'

Meeting Rupert,
Who Is Not Olly

What to do? There's Brexit, yakking away to itself with its thumbs in its waistcoat like some out-of-work barrister practising in front of the mirror in its bedroom, and I'm lying here thinking, do these people not realise that my whole existence as a semi-retired geopolitical boundary is now in question?

It turns out some of them do, though. They're not all as thick as the neck on Barney's best bull.

This lad turns up one day not long after the referendum looking a bit shifty – but too well-dressed for diesel-laundering.

'Howareye?' says me, non-committal but friendly, like.

'Ah, hello, are you the Irish Border?' he says. He sounded posh. 'Only, it's rather odd, talking to something invisible.'

'Better than talking to a wall', says me.

'Yes', he says, 'quite so, but we wouldn't want to ...'

'Aye, I'm only messing,' I says. 'What's that in your hand there, fella?'

'My passport. I thought that maybe you'd need to see it, you know, being a border.'

'You've a lot to learn about this border, mate. You don't need it. Nice suit, by the way.'

'Thanks. Actually, I wanted a word. I've been sent on behalf of Her Majesty's Government to ... I suppose ... to negotiate with you.'

'Ok. That's nice. I thought yous had all forgotten about me.'

'We had. Then you tweeted that photo of the elephant and said, "There's me at the Brexit negotiations," and ...'

'They sent you here. I see. Well, if we're going to be negotiating we better get to know each other. What's your name?'

'I'd prefer not to say.'

'Can I call you, oh, I don't know – Olly?'

'What?! NO!! How did you know?'

'What about Mr Robbins?'

'No.'

'If I can't call you Olly then I need a name for you. You look like a Rupert. You look like you went to a school full of Ruperts. You carry yourself like a Jasper, or a Quentin, or a Whimpleberry, or a Rupert. Can I call you Rupert?'

'If you must. Chatham House Rules apply.'

'So no tweeting our discussions then, Rupert?'

'No tweeting.'

'Not even a wee allusion to the fact that such discussions are being mooted?'

'No tweeting.'

'How about if I do it as a fictional dialogue between

the two of us that will be published in a book at a later date, after the time when Brexit is meant to have happened, but when it'll probably still be dragging on tediously?'

'No.'

'There would be interesting digressions from our endless and pointless discussions.'

'I'm not sure we have time for that. Brexit is quite urgent.'

'You're a funny man. We'll all be here for years talking about this. 800 years of Ireland trying to leave Britain is about to be repaid by 800 years of Britain trying to leave Ireland. There's no rush. Alright, Rupert, you go first.'

'We'd like to propose a range of measures which would mean that there is no return to the border, I mean to the you, of the past ... Are you ok?'

'Sorry, I fell asleep. You're being boring. Did you bring ice cream?'

'Ice cream?'

'I can't negotiate without ice cream.'

'You're kidding.'

'I am not. Would you head in to Newry there and get two 99s and then we can negotiate when you get back.'

Rupert got lost in Newry. Maybe he'd have fared better as Olly, or maybe he just didn't know his way around. The 99s were a bit drippy by the time he came back.

'So as I was saying ...'

'Yeah, Olly, sorry to interrupt but you dropped some ice cream on your suit there.'

'It's Rupert. And bugger.'

'Dry cleaning is the only solution, Olly/Rupert.'

'Can we please get back to the negotiations? Now we've been looking at other borders around the world as possible models for how a post-Brexit you could function seamlessly and frictionlessly ...'

I drifted off a bit while he talked.

Jean is a friend of mine from way back. During the darkest of days she'd stop by and we'd put the world to rights and we'd despair and laugh together about the general state of things. After the Good Friday Agreement we ended up talking about normal stuff – vets' bills, the number of Maltesers in a packet, how to avoid PowerPoint presentations, that kind of thing. We've seen good times and bad times. She'd be a philosophical kind of person, in a direct sort of a way. Rupert was still talking when Jean came along, walking her wee dog, and I thought, Jean will help me out here. Rupert's a nice lad but he talks like a dishwasher manual sometimes.

'Hello, Border.'

'How's it going, Jean?'

'Woof.'

'How's it going, wee dog?'

'Who's your man there, talking to himself?'

'He's talking to me, Jean.'

'But you're not listening.'

'I wouldn't say that. Jean, this is Olly.'

'Rupert. We said my name is Rupert.'

'Do you not know your own name?'

'It's a codename, Jean. Olly wants Rupert to be his codename.'

'Olly's a fine name.'

'Can we stick to Rupert?'

'Nice suit, Rupert.'

'That's what I said, Jean.'

'You know it's got a stain on it?'

'He does.'

'Would it be ok if we got back to negotiations, Border?'

'Is this a Brexit thing, Border?'

'Oh yes, very secret. Rupert-who-used-to-be-Olly has been sent by the British government. Jean's good on the subject of Brexit, Rupert. You should listen to her.'

'This Brexit thing is desperate bad, Rupert.'

'It's unseemly, Jean, that's what it is.'

'Unseemly's the word, Border.'

'Scundering for us all.'

'Scundering, Jean.'

'I don't really understand.'

'We know, Rupert.'

'I'll be back soon, Border.'

'Fair play, Rupert. You can get that suit cleaned in Newry, you know.'

'He's gone, Border.'

'He'll be back. What are you reading there, Jean?'

'It's a kids' book. I'm off to see the nephews.'
'Is it a good one?'
'It's ok. It's called *The EUffalo*.'
'Would you read me it, Jean? It'd calm me down.'
'I'm not sure it will, but ok ...'

A border took a stroll through a deep, dark wood
Liam Fox saw the border and the border looked good
'Where are you going to, little soft border?
Come and play a role in my new world order'
'It's terribly kind of you, Fox, but no
I'm going to have lunch with a EUffalo.'

'A EUffalo? What's a EUffalo?'
'A EUffalo? Why, didn't you know?
It has Donald Tusk, and free trade laws,
And the ECJ at the end of its claws'
'Where are you meeting it?'
'Here by these rocks.
And its favourite food is roasted Fox.'

A border took a stroll through a deep, dark wood
A May saw the border and the border looked good
'Where are you going to, seamless frontier?
Can you be solved by the end of this year?'
'It's really not possible, May, you know
I hear more sense from the EUffalo.'

'A EUffalo? What's a EUffalo?'
'A EUffalo? Why, didn't you know?

It has a flag and a customs union.
(It nearly had a constitution)'
'Where are you meeting it?'
'Here by this hay.
And its favourite food is pickled May.'

'Aw, that's nice, Jean. The nephews'll love it.'
'I'd say so, Border. Isn't it a grand evening, now?'
'I've always specialised in sunsets, Jean.'
'That you have ... Do you think you'll do grand sunsets after Brexit, Border?'
'I will, Jean. But maybe for a while, not so ...'
'Luminescent, Border?'
'Not so luminescent, Jean. Not for a while.'
'Goodnight, Border.'
'Goodnight, Jean.'
'Woof.'
'Night night, wee dog.'
Off she went. And the wee dog. And silence descended.

Some night you should come here, lay yourself down beside me and put your ear to the sod. Then you can listen quietly to the voices of the things that are buried, shallow and deep, within me, and you will learn from the yarns they spin, and the sadnesses they recall, and the wisdom they speak. Then, if you don't know it already, you'll see why I'm so pissed off with Rupert and his Brexit.

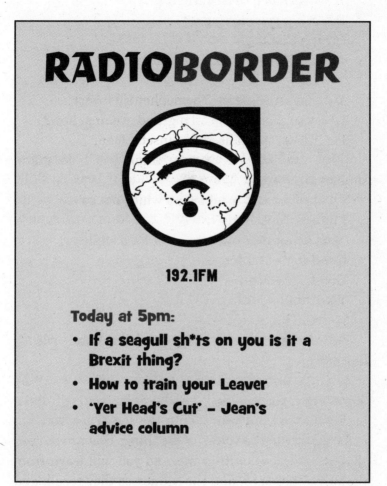

RADIOBORDER

192.1FM

Today at 5pm:

- If a seagull sh*ts on you is it a Brexit thing?
- How to train your Leaver
- 'Yer Head's Cut' – Jean's advice column

Still Here, Jim?

Jim was still here. Where else would he be, I suppose? He had nowhere to Leave to, no hidden Leaving skills that he had suddenly unleashed, no map which would take him on the path to Leaving. No, Jim's Leaving now involved being very unLeft.

'Border.'

'Jim.'

'This is quite boring, isn't it?'

'...'

'Did you ever hear tell of a lad called Samuel Beckett, Border?'

'Oh aye. Went to school round here. Quiet lad. Why do you ask?'

'It passes the time, Border.'

'It would have passed anyway, Jim.'

'...'

'Still Leaving, Jim?'

'Still Leaving, Border.'

'Ok, Jim.'

Jim can stand there for hours, days, weeks on end, in the process of Leaving. I admire his persistence.

'Are you looking forward to Leaving, Jim?'

'Oh yes.'

'Why's that, Jim? Is it the prospect of freedom? The journey into the unknown? The horizons of expectation which you can push back, finding endless potentiality within yourself and your fellow Leavers?'

'No, it's the weather, Border.'

'The weather?'

'It's going to be sunny when I've Left, Border.'

'Sunny uplands?'

'Yes, Border, that's it, I think. Sundry uphills.'

'Sunny uplands, Jim. When you Leave there will be sunny uplands.'

'That's it. I'm Leaving for sunken funlands.'

'Ok, Jim.'

Time for Jim to get into a telephone box and put on the Brexitman suit that Jean knitted for him.

Croissants and Pasties

I saw Jean hurrying towards me one evening in an awful rush, with the wee dog being dragged along behind her on the lead, bouncing off the footpath with the eyes bulging and the claws click-clacketing on the tarmac. Jean was fairly panting by the time she got to me, and the wee dog was disgusted with life.

'Border,' she says.

'I'm here, Jean.'

'I know that,' says Jean. 'Oh, I haven't a breath on me, Border.'

'Is something wrong, Jean? Is Strabane vanished again?'

'No. No, Border, that was fog. No, I was watching the news there and was just about to put the wee dog's dinner in front of it ...'

I looked at the wee dog. The wee dog definitely remembered the dinner not actually getting to the front of it.

'... and the man on the news said there's a delegation from the EU coming to visit you tomorrow.'

'There's never a day goes by but some lad in a suit

comes along and gets his picture taken beside me, pointing, or standing with one foot either side of me. And I never look up, Jean, I never look up.'

'I know, Border, and you are to be praised for your restraint. But that man on the news said that tomorrow it's Monsieur Barnier.'

'Well, now, amn't I glad I got my grass cut this week, Jean? And sure, by tomorrow afternoon I can do a good trim and tidy and be ready. It's a big deal, all the same.'

'But, Border, the man on the news said Monsieur Barnier is coming for a "working breakfast".'

There was a silence. I looked at Jean. She looked at me. The wee dog looked at Jean. And then at me. And me and Jean said together:

'CROISSANTS!'

'Jean, where in the name of hell and all that's holy are we going to get croissants for Michel Barnier's breakfast? It's 7.13pm the night before he arrives and we're standing in a field outside Muff.'

'That's a fair question, Border. The good shops are shut. The shops that are open are croissant-free zones. We could get a sliced pan handily enough in a petrol station.'

'Jean, if I give Michel Barnier toasted sliced pan and peanut butter for breakfast he'll have customs posts on me before he's back in Brussels. And who would blame him?'

'Woof.'

'What's she saying, Jean?'

'Woof woof woof woof woof woof.'

'The wee dog says she'll go and find a breakfast suitable for the EU's Chief Brexit Negotiator and his team.'

The wee dog was going round in circles now. 'Off you go, wee dog,' I said, 'find some exquisite pastries. Also, freshly squeezed orange juice. And probably muesli.' And off she scampered.

Jean went home and I settled down for the night, but I knew I'd not sleep. I was worrying about becoming a hard border. I was worried about meeting Barnier and having to make my case to him and to remember all that stuff about tariffs and checks. I had to remember to ask him about the SPS, and to plead with him that I not end up too proximate to chickens or the internal workings of ruminants. Most of all, I was worried about the croissants. I felt that my future probably depended on the croissants.

At about eleven I heard the distinctive lolloping of Jean's wee dog, its name tag rattling as it ran, its ears pinned back in the bordery wind as it tore towards me – with a blue plastic shopping bag in its mouth. Thon's some mutt, I thought to myself, though as she got closer I began to feel a little sceptical about the shape of the bag. Still, I thought, croissants in Muff near midnight. That would be a miracle. Miracles are in short supply where Brexit is concerned, as you may have noticed yourself. 'Grand job, wee dog. Tip out the croissants there,' I said, 'til we have an inspection.'

The dog tipped up the bag. Custard Creams. Bourbons. Jammie Dodgers. And all of them, not to put too fine a point on it, a bit slobbery.

I looked at the wee dog. She was delighted with herself. 'Is this what you got me for the breakfast, wee dog?'

She assented, in a wee doggy way. 'Wee dog, I am grateful for your help, truly I am. But this is not a breakfast fit for the EU's Chief Brexit Negotiator. He's a man of sophisticated tastes. Leaving aside the canine saliva in which they are marinated, the contents of a box of Family Circle biscuits are not how he would choose to begin his day, and I need him to be in a good mood, otherwise it's physical infrastructure for me and rabies injections for you [technically this wasn't true but I had to put the frighteners on the mutt]. Did you just go home and steal these biscuits from Jean's cupboard?' The wee dog said nothing. 'Wee dog, please take these back and, if you can, find me some croissants. They're like puff pastry things.' The dog went off, a bit more slowly than before and I felt that my hopes of putting on an impressive continental breakfast had probably gone with it.

I must have fallen asleep for a while. I dreamt that David Davis was dressed in a devil costume and riding around on a souped-up lawnmower trying to find me so he could cut my grass. And some time, probably around midnight, was when it must have happened. I'm not proud of this, dear reader, but you must understand it was an accident. Somewhere, along the length of me, and I'm a bit hazy on the details, a lorry 'shed its load', as they say on the radio, and the load was, I believe, kegs of beer. I woke up with a start and a surprise and I was, I think it is fair to say, absolutely plastered.

I do not recall much of the rest of the evening. I know the wee dog came back with another bag. I spoke to it fondly, if a little incoherently. I may have said that it was the best f***ing dog in the whole f***ing world and if anyone said otherwise they'd have me to deal with because there's no other dog I'd rather have as a border's best friend than you wee dog you lovely wee dog c'mere 'til I give you a pet but don't be lifting your f***ing leg near me.

I know I sent Jean a few texts, because I saw them on my iPad the next morning:

Thursday 00:15

> oh Jean a lorrrydropped a keg on me an it split so it did n I think I might be a bit ahhm pissed or something xx border

Delivered

Thursday 00:23

> it seeeeeeped in I couldnt held it help it fing autocorrect

Delivered

I love you jean you are my best friend like did I ever tell you I love you but god I hate brexit

Delivered

I mean Brexit whats it like a big pile of crap but sure I have you your my best friend. oh wait the wee dogs here

Delivered

the wee dog brought the croissants Jean it's a wonderdog so it is i'm going to kiss yer dog

Delivered

might boke see u in morning bring jam

Delivered

You know the way, when you wake in the morning with a bit of a hangover – let's call it for what it was – you know that way, and nothing much is working except your sense of smell, but it's working overtime because everything else is taking the day off? Well, my sense of smell was telling me that whatever was in that bag had come from the general area of Macari's chipper. I nudged the wee dog. It woke up slowly and it did that dog thing where they stretch their legs out in front of them like they're going to catapult themselves into dogland. When she'd wandered off for a leg-lift and come back I says to her, 'Wee dog, is there any chance we're at cross-purposes here with the croissants? Maybe show me what's in the bag, because it sure doesn't smell like the best Parisian viennoiserie pastry to me.'

The dog looks indignant and tips out the contents of the bag as if to prove how well she's done. Oh My Sweet Lord. Pasties. Not pastries. Pasties.

Now, it occurs to me that some of you may not be familiar with the pastie. A traditional dish of Belfast, but available elsewhere in Northern Ireland, and beyond – though not far beyond, for who would want it? – the pastie is traditionally made from pork mince, with potato, onion and some spices, moulded into a substantial burger shape and then covered in batter and deep fried. Usually it is eaten in the 'pastie supper' form, that is with chips, and usually when the consumer of the pasty is pissed, because otherwise you might pause to think about what you're eating, what's in it, and what it actually tastes like. A croissant it is not.

'Right,' I said, though 'right' didn't really reflect what I was thinking. The wee dog was sniffing the pasties and seemed ready to tuck in. Jean appeared.

'Pastie suppers, Border?'

'Pastie suppers, Jean.'

'The wee dog thought you said pasties, didn't it?'

'So it would seem, Jean.'

'Shit.'

'*Ah, bonjour, vous êtes la frontière? Et c'est votre ami, Madamoiselle Jean?*'

'*Monsieur Barnier, bonjour. S'il vous plaît, prendre un ... petit déjeuner,* I guess.'

'We can speak in English, Border. What an usual breakfast. A local speciality?'

'Erm, yes. Yes, we often have this for *petit déjeuner,* Jean, don't we?'

'Oh aye, at least once a week.'

I had an idea. 'Actually, Monsieur Barnier, we are very concerned that this traditional dish will be threatened by *le Brexit.* It depends, for example, on ahm ... help me out here, Jean ...'

'... on cross-border pigs.'

'Yes, exactly. The distinctive spicy flavour of *la pastie* is achieved by having the pigs criss-cross the border eating herbs from either side of me. And, well, you know yerself, Michel ...'

'*Mais oui, le Brexit* threatens all our livelihoods. I shall do all I can to maintain the tradition of *la pastie,* and everything else about you, Border. I will personally ensure that *la pastie* – like Roquefort, like Champagne – receives the full legal protection afforded by EU regulation. It shall have Protected Designation of Origin status. Now, let me try some of this delicacy.'

You're not going to believe this. He liked it. He took some away with him for his mates in Brussels. I'd say that place fairly smelt of chip grease and vinegar for a few days after he got back. They'll not be forgetting about me over there for a while.

So we had the bantz with Michel and that was all grand. He's on our side, sure we know that, and he was very reassuring about the animal welfare issues.

'You will not be needing the long-armed gloves, *mon ami*,' were his very words.

And he went off happy. As his motorcade purred off towards Dublin I began to really feel the effects of the spilt drink.

'Well, that went well, considering, Border.'

'It did, Jean.'

Brexisnt.

Could I sue Brexit for damages?

**Aye, sure, go on, rain on me, as if that
could make things worse.**

I have a little sign on my desk to remind
me and my visitors of my responsibilities.
It says 'The Backstop's Here'.

Don't let me keep you now.

Ambridge Analytica manipulate
rural voters.

I was going to call this book Fuckoon.

I'm Brexasperated.

The **7**
Habits of Highly Effective Leaving

Jim

World expert on the process of Leaving.
Drawing on three years' experience of
Leaving and going absolutely nowhere

**Special Brexit
edition**

ABOUT THIS BOOK

Do you want to Leave? I mean *really Leave*. Leave absolutely and completely. Leave so there's no coming back. Yes? Good for you. Me too.

My name's Jim and I'm a Leaver. I've been Leaving since 2016. I've put in at least 25,000 hours of Leaving over the past few years and now I've distilled my vast experience into a book so you too can be a Leaver. A BeLeaver.

There are seven steps to Leaving:

1. You must BeLeave in BeLeaving.
2. Tell yourself you're going to Leave. Don't think about how, just tell yourself that it's going to be easy.
3. Tell everyone else you're going to Leave. If they object, tell them they're Leaving with you whether they like it or not.
4. Find a safe place from which to Leave.
5. Stand in that place.
6. Wait. Something will come along soon.
7. Be calm. Becalmed.

In this book I'll take you through the 7 steps and then you'll be ready to Leave. You'll be standing, becalmed, alongside me. I know you're excited about standing around saying you're going to Leave and not actually Leaving. I am too.

Let's Leave! Soon! Really soon!

Curse Like a Border

'Rupert, you're back. I see you got the suit cleaned.'

Rupert had a laptop with him this time. He's all business, bless him.

'So, Border, we have modelled your future based on scenarios associated with existing frontier arrangements in comparator border situations.'

'You've been looking at other borders.'

'Yes.'

'You've been looking at other borders that I could be like.'

'Exactly.'

'And there aren't any.'

'Not exactly, no. However, we have ...'

'I've been doing some research too.'

And so I had. These Brexit bozos think I'm thick, but I hadn't been sleeping on the job. As soon as I realised this stupid Brexit idea would mean I might have to go back to work I started texting around the other borders I knew to find out what the story with contemporary bordering is, because I'm a bit out of practice. Borders, it has to be said, and it pains me to say it, are

44

not the nicest of entities, and the only one I ever got on with was the Berlin Wall and we all know what happened there.

I'd heard the Gibraltar–Spain Border was going to be as badly affected by Brexit as me. So, I thought, border solidarity. I texted it to see if it was ok:

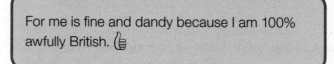

For me is fine and dandy because I am 100% awfully British.

Delusional. It just goes to show that many of the arbitrarily imposed geopolitical dividing lines around the world attended the same English bordering school. And when I pointed this out it just pretended it didn't know me.

Lo siento, nuevo teléfono. ¿Quién es este?

The Korean Border had been in the news, and it's a proper border. It wasn't very helpful, though:

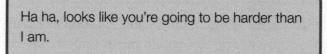

Ha ha, looks like you're going to be harder than I am.

Lots of the Brexiters were talking about how I could be like the Swiss Border. They seem to think everything just flows over the Swiss Border without a bit of trouble.

That's not true, of course. And the Swiss Border is very smug:

> Really? People and goods cross me all the time. It's complicated but kinda fun, you know, all the languages and chat and so on.

Being the Swiss Border is not a proper job, it's a skiing holiday.

I showed all these texts to Rupert. He told me his boss reckoned I could be like the US–Canada Border.

'Rupert,' I said, 'when we were at bordering school the US–Canada Border called me Paddy and did a fake jig every time it saw me. Very embarrassing for all concerned.' But Rupert was insistent, so I texted the US–Canada Border to find out what it's like being a fully fledged international border with nutcases on one side of you:

> Is that just physical infrastructure or are you just happy to see me?

> Ha ha.

It was always a sarcastic border. I persisted:

No, really, what's it like?

Wackos with guns and dope and border guards with serious weaponry. You'll love it, dude.

Sounds exciting.

'Rupert, I'm getting worried now.'

'Well, ok, what about the Norway–Sweden Border?'

'Yes, nice border. Suave, interesting. I'll text it.'

The next day Rupert was back. 'Well, Border, did Norway–Sweden get back to you?'

'Yup. I asked it was true it had no checks and no physical infrastructure, like you said. Look.'

No, I have many checks plus I have nice Swedish and Norwegian peoples either side of me, whereas you have …

Yeah I know, I know …

'Ah. I see.'

'And, Rupert, I've also been texting the US–Mexico Border.'

'We don't really see that as a useful analogy.'

'I bet you don't. It told me it saw Boris Johnson on TV.'

> Yo dude snap on the hairy-headed dumbass demagogue!

'Referring, I assume, to a physical resemblance between our Foreign Secretary and future Prime Minister and the President of the United States.'

'So it would seem. And it had some advice for me in how to deal with you, Rupert.'

> Tell them they don't own you, dude, and you're gonna bite them on their dumb asses.

> Ok. I'm not sure I have the nerve but I'll think about it.

'What about Monaco?'

'Monaco? Yes, of course. I'm just like the Monegasque Border, you know, Rupert. I've the Aughnacloy Grand Prix, and the Art Deco casino in Faughart, and that tax-avoiding, multi-millionaire dairy farmer in Omeath ...'

'I see your point, Border. I'll be back soon.'

Jean came along with the wee dog. 'I passed Rupert there. He's a sad-looking character today.'

'He wanted to compare me to other borders, Jean.'

'Comparisons are odious, Border.'

'That's Wilde, Jean.'

'Here, Border, did you hear about those English tourists driving around Ken's field this morning?'

'I did, Jean. They had the map upside down.'

'Oh right.'

'Yer man driving shouts, "We have decided on the route we are taking and we are sticking to it no matter what. There is no going back!"'

'I heard they were headed to the river.'

'Straight in, Jean. Splash.'

'It's cold this time of year. Good night, Border.'

'Cheerio, Jean.' And off she went. I am well accustomed to the curlew's lonely cry, the raven's dark and melancholy call, the bleat of terror from a lost lamb, cold and trembling on the mountainside, but not one of these is as forlorn as the sound of Rupert trying to find a way to make Brexit actually work. He said to me one day, 'Border, Brexit is simple.' Jeez, he fairly regretted that.

'Forgive me a moment of intemperate language here, Rupert the Brexit,' says me, 'but IT'S NOT F***ING "SIMPLE". Why does never a day pass without someone telling me, "Oh, it's simple"? It's not.

It's complicated. Brexit is f***ing complicated. When you say it's "simple" you're one of the reasons it's complicated. Imagine, Ruperto, imagine if Brexit day came, and happened despite all my warnings, and imagine I unleashed an ancient curse that had been entrusted to my geological strata by the druids, and that the skies did darken and moan, and clamour was rampant, and strife did thus reign amongst the nations. Would you still be saying, "Brexit is simple"?'

'Well, under those circumstances probably not ...'

'So don't say it at all then.'

'Is that true, though?'

'The curses and the druids and the strife? Oh yes, Rupert, it's well known around these parts, that ancient curse.'

'It's quite frightening.'

'Maybe you're not used to curses, Rupert. I've been working on some Brexit curses. Do you want to hear them?'

'Not really, I'd prefer to get on to discussing trade and tariff collection, if that's ...'

Well, now, I don't like being diverted. I may look a bit squiggly and uncertain of my direction on a map but I'm pretty much a straight line when I've decided on something.

'Rupy,' says I, 'you're going to hear the curses. Here goes:

You're a heap of shite so big you throw a shade over the Mourne mountains. You're a moral chasm so empty

50

you echo deeper than the Marble Arch caves. You've more faces than a barn of chickens. There aren't enough blades of grass along my length to number the curses I cast upon you.

May your milk curdle, your livestock escape, your ATM always tell you you've insufficient funds. May your bubbles always burst just before they separate from that wee stick thing that has the loop on the end of it. May your ice cream only ever be sorbet.

I pray fervently that your biros are all chewed at the ends and leak in your pocket; that your tractor is difficult to get the parts for. You're a slabber, a goon, a muckraker, a hallion, an unpicker of seams. You're a get-off-the-bus-without-thanking-the-driver.

When you open your Taytos and the packet bursts and crisps fall all over the carpet, that was me. When your Wi-Fi is slow, your pint less full than you thought, your chicken juices not flowing clear when pierced with a fork, your hot water bottle leaking a bit in the bed – all of that is my ire.

A curse upon yer telescope held to the unseeing eye, yer Excel sheet brain, yer swaggery masquerade of learning. And a curse of curses fall down on that shudder of repulsion you hold so dear. May the loathing you've nurtured turn upon you, ravenous, and feed on your entrails.

Backstop

'Jean.'

'Border.'

'Woof.'

'Wee dog. Ahm, Jean?'

'Yes, Border.'

'Jean, what's the wee dog wearing?'

'It's a backstop, Border. They're all the rage.'

'What's it for, Jean? She looks like she stuck her head up an ice cream cone and got no flake.'

'It's well you should ask, Border, because you'll need to know. In the case of the wee dog, she had an operation on her nether regions and the backstop is to prevent her from doing damage to herself. You know what dogs are like for that. You have to put measures in place because they can't be trusted.'

'She looks a bit daft. And miserable.'

'You'll have heard, no doubt, that the EU are worried that Brexit will mean a profound change to your function which would not be in keeping with the letter, spirit and intention of the Good Friday/Belfast Agreement and a threat to the integrity of the Single Market?'

'Oh, aye.'

'And that the Irish government is particularly exercised about this.'

'Understandably, because their wee bit of a field comes right up to the boundary here.'

'And so they have agreed a backstop.'

'To stop Brexit picking at its nether regions?'

'Exactly.'

'And do you think I need a backstop, Jean?'

'Border,' she says, 'you know that lad who lives next door to me who likes to think he's a Formula 1 driver in his wee Skoda of a Saturday evening?'

'I do, Jean,' says I.

'Well, I tried talking to him,' says Jean. 'And I tried talking to his parents. But he still does the donuts outside the house and near takes the paint off my car. So I rang my insurance company and says I to them, "Insurance company, you'd better give me a full backstop, because the lad next door is not to be trusted behind the wheel of a vehicle." So that's like the backstop, Border,' she says.

'To stop your neighbours destroying everything because there's no talking to them?' says I.

'That's it, Border,' says Jean. 'I mean, if you lived in

the flat next door to a pyromaniac wouldn't you put in a good sprinkler system as a backstop?'

'I would.'

'So what does the backstop do, Jean? I mean actually do.'

'It keeps Northern Ireland very EU, but not actually EU. It keeps the rest of the UK a bit EU, so they have to pretend harder that they're not actually EU. But, to be honest now, it's possible pretending harder will be too hard for the rest of the UK, so they might just pretend the same way as Northern Ireland.'

'I've no idea what you're talking about, Jean.'

Well, Jean went on for a while, telling me about the time she was at the airport and she saw the baggage handlers with her bag. One wanted to put it on one plane, another on a different plane and one was going to leave it on the tarmac and sell it later. 'I thought to myself, thank God for backstop travel insurance,' she said.

Jean showed me a picture in a book of a wee lad who had been out skating on a pond because all his mates had told him it would be fine but he'd fallen into the icy water and a man had laid a ladder out over the ice and was crawling out to get him, using the ladder to evenly redistribute his weight.

'The man with the ladder is the backstop and the wee lad's mates are Brexit?'

'That's right, Border.'

Now I understood what the backstop was, but I wasn't sure I'd get a backstop, because not everybody around here likes the backstop. Rupert told me the backstop negotiation was the pinnacle of his diplomatic career for nearly ten minutes and then the DUP got on the phone to his boss. So I was wondering, how will them negotiators ever get the backstop past the Brexity people?

For example, the EU and the Irish government said the backstop had to stay in place 'unless and until' something better came along. I was thinking to myself, Jeez, I started out as a temporary arrangement that was only meant to be here unless and until a better one came along. Best not to mention that probably.

I listened to the Brexiters on the radio and they were saying things like:

'Eve plucked the forbidden backstop from the tree of knowledge and look where that got us.'

'Magna Carta specifically prohibits the use of a backstop.'

'Plato banished backstops from his Republic and I see no reason why we should disagree with Plato just because the Aristotelian EU says we have to.'

They started to talk about the backstop as if it was some actual thing. Like the backstop was going to take on a monstrous corporeal form of mythic proportions, rise from the Thames, and with a damp, dripping, clawed and hirsute foot crush the Palaces of Westminster and then settle down in a bungalow outside Strabane and do a bit of celebrity charity work.

I like the backstop myself. I like it because it stops your neighbour sh*tting on your doorstep and then telling you it's your fault for having a doorstep. But you've probably heard tell of the ERG? The European Research Group? They have a terrible name – they're not European, they don't do any research and they all hate each other. Anyway, everybody in Brexitland seems to think the ERG is a great bunch of fellas. And boy-o-boy do they dislike the backstop. If the backstop was playing the fiddle in their back garden they'd close the curtains and turn up the radio.

A funny thing about the ERG is that they're mainly a bunch of fusty oul lads careering into the future with their backs turned towards it as they gaze fondly on a past which is a pile of detritus but which they see as a flag waving proudly against a setting sun. 'Angels of History' is the term, Jean tells me, but let's not get distracted. Anyway, super-exercised by the backstop are the ERG. Apoplectic. You'd nearly worry about them. Nearly.

One day I got a communication from them. I say 'communication', because, as you've seen, I try to keep up with the young people and how they do things. I am a minor Twitter sensation after all. And I do email! The ERG – you're not going to believe this, though maybe you will – sent me a telegram. I hadn't seen one of them for years. The postman who brought it said his da delivered the last one in Cavan in the 1970s and it was

about a bull that had died in service. And he handed
me this:

POST OFFICE
TELEGRAM

EUROPEAN RESEARCH GROUP

@BORDER
IRISH

NO NEED FOR BACKSTOP ABSOLUTE RED

HERRING EXCLAMATION

TECHNOLOGICAL SOLUTION READY SOON STOP
WAITING FOR NEW VALUES AND COPPER COILS STOP
SEND TEA STOP

These lads can't even send a text, and they expect to
replace the backstop with what? Carrier pigeons maybe.
A letter, I thought. I'll type them a letter:

> @BorderIrish,
> The Irish Border,
> Ireland (island of)

Dear ERG,
Thanks for the telegram, lads. What's the thing
about the fish?

Listen, I know yous don't like the backstop but I
think it's a grand idea. It'll save me from crackpots
like yerselves.

I'll explain it with a wee story. This is a story about a field and the things that inhabit it. A story about a man known as the Baron, though whether he merited a mention in Burke's *Peerage*, I never did know.

The Baron was a raggedy sort of being but a sleeked one too, and he accumulated many fields across the counties. One beautiful big field he bought at auction had been farmed for many years by two brothers, and uneasily they worked and lived together, sharing the duties and chores.

The Baron had money enough in his pockets for twenty men but his real currency was strife. He saw these two brothers and saw that their harmony was but a front and underneath that they had simmering ways, each wanting the field for themselves but neither able to take it for himself nor tell the other he wanted it. The Baron, divil the man, took that field and he split it into two unequal parts, giving one part to each of the brothers while whispering foul in their ears.

The Baron's love of hate didn't stop there. Border people know that the Fairythorn tree is never to be moved, never to be dug up, unless you don't mind being cursed and pained. The Baron divided the brothers' field with a row of Fairythorn, thinking they'd never shift it.

And that was how it went. The trees grew, generations grew with them, the brothers, and then the children of the brothers, estranged themselves,

as the generations looked across the Fairythorn
border and knew each other less and less. And then
a strange thing happened. The Baron, now an aged
and decaying shell of a man, was seen in the dead of
night digging up the Fairythorns. The next morning
the trees were gone. There was only a line in the
grass where the Fairythorns had been.

The Baron would tell anyone who asked him,
and many who hadn't, how this came about: 'I was
passing by the field that night, feeling rightly, and
I heard my name being called. So I climbed the
hedge and went in. It's my field, after all. And the
voices calling me were coming from the trees, like
rowdy childer in an unattended schoolroom.'

'I got to the Fairythorns and I felt a hundred
clawing hands on my back, and a hundred more
pulling my hair, and a hundred more scratching my
face, and they all three hundred shouting "Dig up
the thorns, Baron!"'

'"I will not!" I said. But then they scratched and
pulled harder and I saw, opening up in the ground
in front of me, a freshly dug plot and one of the
voices said, "That'll be your grave, Baron, if you
don't dig up the thorns this night." So dig I did,
with the fear of God in me.'

The thorns were gone and the field restored,
though it had that scar across the land.

And the funny thing is now, my ERG friends,
one day I myself had seen the great-grandchild
of one of the original brothers scattering flowers

on the scar and I had said to her, 'What are ye at?'

And she had said, 'I'll tell you, Border. I got fed up of not seeing my cousins, but you know you can't dig up the thorns because of the things that inhabit them. So I went one evening to see them things, and I brought them sweets and ice cream, and I told them the Baron had put them there for the sake of foul division.'

'The things in the trees didn't know this and they said to me, "You're brave to come here with this story. Leave the Baron to us." And they called him in that night. And now I come to give them flowers and sweets. And raspberry ripple.'

So that's why the Baron was taken one night by the things that live in the field to dig up the Fairythorns and make the field border invisible. So the wee children could talk to each other without division. And the man or woman that puts that division back would be well advised to take cognisance of what happened to the Baron, for it could happen to them too, and to be shown the plot of your own demise is a fierce frightening thing, and more so if your arrogance stops you seeing it 'til the last minute. And that's why, when you look over that hedge there, in the field you'll see a scar in the grass. And if you listen carefully you might hear that line in the field telling stories about itself in letters and on Twitter.

All the best now, and watch out,
Irish Border

60

The ERG might not understand my sentience, but the EU does. They know I'm not just a line in the grass. I have feelings, and those feelings now deserve to be respected. Well, the EU, they're the quare crafty lads, so they are. What they did was, when they realised the ERG didn't like the backstop they said to themselves, 'We know, we'll take the backstop and we'll split it up into wee parts.' It's a bit like what Hughie Murphy does when the taxman comes to inspect his farm. 'Where's your silage baler?' says the taxman. 'For depreciation calculation purposes you must declare any farm machinery you have on the premises.' 'Ah, Holy God, sure I don't have one of them,' says Hughie. 'Are you sure?' says the taxman, looking at fifty perfectly wrapped bales of silage a-shining in the sun. 'Oh, aye,' says Hughie. And what Hughie has done is take his baler apart for tax purposes and hid the bits around the yard. Then, when the taxman's gone he reassembles it.

So what the EU did was they hid the parts of the backstop in different pages of a big book called the Withdrawal Agreement. Now, to be honest, you'd be driven mad trying to read the whole Withdrawal Agreement looking to find the bits of the backstop, because it reads like it was written by a solicitor after he'd had a few jars. But that was the point. The EU was thinking, nobody will be able to find the backstop before they have to have a vote on it. It'll be like doing *Where's Wally?* on Christmas Day – all the Brexiters will give up and watch the Queen and fall asleep.

But no – the EU underestimated all them Brexiters. Even when the backstop was split up into tiny wee parts and hidden in a big compendium of incomprehensibility, them bloody Brexiters could smell it. If you hid it in a silage pit and covered it with tyres they'd find it. They refused to be taken in by the backstop

Talking of solicitors, Rupert had me confused with all the backstop talk. So I wrote to Bernie to get his expert opinion on the matter. He replied:

⚖ Bernie McFadden & Co
Solicitors, so we are

Newry and Border Area Branch

3.12.18

Dear Border,
How are ye? How's Jean?

Here, you were looking for legal advice. I'd say, houl on to the Backstop like a fox houls on to a chicken. And don't be trusting them f███ing Brexiters an inch, for them's the boys would sell their own grannies for a piece of pie and a lick of sugar.

Cheers now,
Bernie

That cleared that up. I showed the letter to Jean, and we agreed that Bernie has some legal head on him.

Jean says to me, 'Border, it's always a good idea to book your holiday before you pack your bags. I mean, who in their right mind would head to the airport with the whole family and no flights booked, no hotel sorted, no spending money with them and no idea where they're going?'

'Alright, will you be backstop in the morning, Jean?'

'Yes. See you then, Border.'

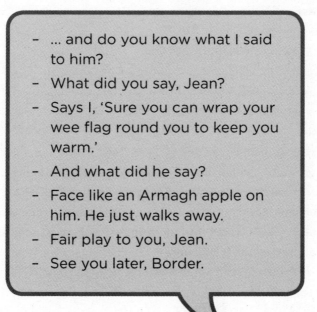

- ... and do you know what I said to him?
- What did you say, Jean?
- Says I, 'Sure you can wrap your wee flag round you to keep you warm.'
- And what did he say?
- Face like an Armagh apple on him. He just walks away.
- Fair play to you, Jean.
- See you later, Border.

J-J-J-Jim

Winter. As evening falls there is a gentle sparkle on my grass, the first frosts of the season, like a sign that there is another world trying to signal to us, from a place the old folk might once have called the fairy world. Talking of which, Jim is still here. I look at him now and again and feel a sense of pity. He's also starting to get very irritating.

'Are you ok there, Jim?'

'Oh aye, no bother, Border.'

'Alright. Well, I'm going to sleep soon, Jim.'

'Goodnight, Border. I'm Leaving.'

'I know ... So you'll still be here tomorrow morning, Jim?'

'I will. But I'm Leaving. Brrrrrrr.'

'Are you cold, Jim? It's a fair cool night.'

'N-n-n-not c-c-cold.'

'Have you no coat?'

'I'm w-w-wrapped in my n-n-n-newly regained s-s-s-sovereignty, so I am.'

'It doesn't seem to be keeping you very warm.'

'I'm L-L-L-Leaving, B-B-Border.'

'I heard that. Ok, Jim.'

Chequers

It was some time in 2018. I can't recall the date. Rupert turned up one day with his unconvincing negotiation face on him. He had a lever-arch file the size of a piglet under his arm. We're for some day of it today, I thought to myself.

'Well, Rupert,' I said. 'What's it to be today?'

'Border, I'd like to talk to you about a Facilitated Customs Arrangement. Do you have PowerPoint facilities here?'

'In a field on the Monaghan–Armagh Border, Rupert? Aye, hang on a minute. Or would you like to use Prezi? Or maybe Keynote if you have a Mac?'

'Keynote would be great, actually.'

'I was being sarcastic. There isn't even a table here. What's on your mind, Rupert?'

'Well, I had hoped to show you some diagrams. It's all rather complicated. We call it a Facilitated Customs Arrangement because ...'

'Let me guess. It facilitates customs arrangements.'

'Yes. How did you know?'

'And you call it that because there is no catchy name for it?'

'Yes.'

'And there's no catchy name for it because no one else, anywhere in the world, does it?'

'Yes, that's more or less true.'

'And no one else does it because it's stupid?'

'I wouldn't say that.'

'And its entire construction as a scheme is based around the United Kingdom government trying to appease the right wing of the Conservative Party while recognising that there is actually a real world out there too?'

'That's one way of looking at it. We're hoping to have our own customs system overlapping with the EU's so that we can collect tariffs due to the EU and pass those on. Now, this means a new and rather interesting ...'

'Rupert, do we have to do this today?'

'Well, Border, you see the cabinet is meeting at Chequers tomorrow to discuss it, so I hoped we might come to some agreement ahead of that.'

'Rupert, I like you. I enjoy talking to you, most of the time. You can be a bit boring now and again. But you're a nice fella with a terrible job. You get sent here with these plans from your government and they're never actually plans, they're just ... Well, it's like you all decided in mid-life that you were going to learn piano, and you booked yourselves a gig to play Beethoven's Emperor Concerto at the Royal Albert Hall in the Proms, and you sold out all the tickets, and did the press interviews, but none of you ever actually learned to play the piano.'

Rupert bridled. 'It's a tricky negotiation but we have the upper hand.'

'You don't. It's like the time Jean's neighbour said he was opening a nightclub and Jean said what about the noise and yer man said you or the council will have to put in noise prevention it's nothing to do with me. He thought he had the upper hand in the negotiations.'

'What happened?'

'Jean bulldozed his house, so that fixed that.'

'I sense that you are angry about Brexit, Border, but still, couldn't we discuss some changes to the Common Travel Area arrangements ...'

'Rupert, stop. It's time for me to go see your boss.'

'What do you mean?'

'I mean, f*** it, I'm going to Chequers.'

'Border, you can't ... Border? Border!'

For the past twenty or so years I've been an invisible border. If anyone asks, I'll tell them that my invisibility is perfectly poised between two political ideologies – one can pretend I'm not there and the other can pretend I am, and both can think they're right. Genius! In reality, having persuaded everyone that I am (a) invisible and (b) crucial to the maintenance of the fragile consensus, I can actually take time off and no one notices. Who's going to miss an invisible border? I spent three weeks in Australia in 2009. No complaints were received. I went on a yoga retreat in India in 2014. So a quick trip over to Chequers wasn't going to be a problem. Jean covers for me if there's ever a problem, but there never is.

So I booked my ticket to Stansted.

My geography of England is a bit vague, to be honest, but once I find a county boundary, I can slither along it pretty quick. Buckinghamshire is where Chequers is. Buckinghamshire has very neat hedges, big, perfect square fields and well-behaved crops. It looks like someone obsessive has tidied up County Down. I got a bit lost. At a service station I stopped in for an ice cream and there in the car park were all these lads on motorbikes, the big kind with the low-down seats. When they had their hands on the handlebars they looked like wee kids trying to see over the sweety counter. I rarely break from my disguise because, you can imagine, it upsets people, but I was a bit desperate to get to Chequers on time and these lads looked like they knew the road.

'Howareye there, lads,' I said, wheeling my bag

along. Now usually when I take on my grassy look and talk there's a bit of explaining to do, but these lads took it in their stride. Off came the helmets. The big lad at the front says to me, 'Are you the Irish Border?'

'Aye,' says I. 'And I'm trying to get to Chequers to have a word with the Prime Minister because, no harm to yous, she's an eejit.'

And do you know, they all took off their helmets, and, like one of those flash mob things, they all went down on one knee and lifted their helmets above their heads and sang in unison, 'LIKE A SINNER BEFORE THE GATES OF HEAVEN I'LL COME CRAWLING ON BACK TOOOO YOU!'

'Like Brexit, you mean?' I said. And they all nodded. The big guy said, 'Chequers is that way,' pointing, and they put their helmets on and rode off. Takes all sorts.

It was a big house, with a drive like a corridor, and men talking into their shirt cuffs, and dogs. Dogs everywhere, and not wee dogs. Oh no. Big dogs. Big, ugly, nasty dogs with noses that could sniff out a border, a backstop or a European passport at a hundred yards. I had to go full invisibility to get in and even then the smell of the raspberry ripple I'd had for lunch had the dogs on the go.

When you get inside, though, Chequers is a bit disappointing. The people must have been smaller when it was built because it's all a bit cramped, and twee, like your auntie's best room, but bigger. Musty too.

I hid in a plant pot in what I took to be the main room. I thought, they've been more or less ignoring me for two years now so even if I did a dance, recited some poetry and sprinkled curses on their heads, they'd probably only think somebody left a door open and there was a bit of a draft. Jean had told me that if I was rumbled I was to shout, 'Huzzah for Brexit!' and while they were all shouting it back I could get out. (Apparently 'Huzzah!' is English for 'Yeeeeooooo!')

The plant pot had been nicely watered so I was happy in there. And then, would you believe it, the Prime Minster came in to the room with a folder with all her Brexit notes and that in it, and she put it down and started practising her spiel for later. Off she went with, 'I'm very clear ...' and, I tell you, in about ten seconds I was fast asleep. When I woke up she was gone. I thought, that's some soporific facility you have there, Missus May. I see how you've come a long way in your career.

There was a clinking of lunch things from the other room and talking and laughing. Then David Davis and Boris Johnson came in. I had a natural urge to jump out and confront them, but I held my nerve and earwigged. I'd seen Davis doing a speech in Germany the week before. He'd been telling the Europeans, very slowly so they'd understand him, that a technological solution to me was easy.

'So I told them,' he was saying to Boris, 'I have a robot lawnmower from Sweden that cuts my grass when I'm not in Yorkshire. If that kind of technology works horticulturally, how hard can it be to patrol the border?'

'A robocop from Yorkshire, Davis? Excellent. British technology at the forefront of the world, eh?'

How did these people ever control so much of the globe? I'm embarrassed to be connected to them sometimes.

So they all started gathering in the room. Philip Hammond was there, the Chancellor of the Exchequer. He doesn't look like a man who's enjoying himself much. I was reminded of the time there was a circus pulled up in Lifford and they had camels and one of them escaped and wandered the border trying to look dignified but you could tell it was sh*tting itself.

Anyway, they're all jabberjabber: 'A woman came into my office to ask about a dog licence but actually she wanted to talk about tariff-free trade'; or 'My PPS told me the other day that my breakfast yoghurt has been across 162 borders before I eat it. Extraordinary!'; or, 'Do we actually own Donegal, or done gall, or whatever it's called?'

Off they went, talking. They talked about everything except me. But at the same time, they were kind of talking about me. Because every solution someone came up with, they'd all go, 'That's it!' and then Rupert, sitting up behind the Prime Minister, would say something like, 'I'm afraid we are forgetting the Irish Border,' and they'd all go, 'Ah, yes,' or worse, and then they'd start to argue. Davis got very agitated. I thought to myself, this man's on the edge. And I should know. He turned round at one point and looked straight at me.

'Did anyone see that plant pot move?' he said.

'David, you're losing it. Focus on how we can reduce our payment to the dastardly EU.'

'I'm sure I saw it move. I remember from my SAS training ...'

'Reserve SAS, David.'

'... from my Reserve SAS training that the Russkis would hide in plant pots before leaping out and assassinating our chaps.'

'You're suggesting that there's a Russian spy in the plant pot?'

'An EU spy, Prime Minster.'

'Have some cake, David.'

They argued away with themselves and all they really agreed was to come back next time and if a solution hadn't been found to Brexit they would have a séance and ask Pitt the Younger.

'Or Jacob Rees-Mogg,' said one of them.

'Same thing,' said another, and they all laughed and went home, leaving only the Prime Minister in the room. This was my chance.

I jumped out of the pot. 'How's it going there, Theresa?'

She couldn't see me but, just instinctively, like, she said, 'I'm very clear ...'

'No, I'm very clear. In fact I'm invisible, which is the whole point.'

There was a bit of to and fro, but she's a slippery one and by the end of it she just kept saying, 'We're taking back control of our money, our laws and our borders ...'

and I'd say, 'Ahem, I don't think so on the last one there,' and we agreed to call it a day.

I went back to where I belong, convinced that I was totally f***ed if these people were going to stay in charge of Brexit. I heard on the news that David Davis resigned the next day. He sent me a nice text message:

You useless line on the map you stubborn bastard you did this on purpose my whole fucking career led to this and you grassy shit you've ruined it you haven't heard the last of this I was in the SAS you know

Bernie McFadden & Co

Solicitors, so we are

Newry and Border Area Branch

24.1.19

Dear Brexit,
How's it going? C'mere to me, I've been
instructed by my client the British Border
in Ireland (aka The Irish Border) that you're
being an awful f██████ing pain in the arse, so
you are. This isn't great now and since there's
no sign of yous halting this nuisance,
I am hereby issuing you with notice that
we'll see your ass in court, as they say
on
the American telly.

Cheers now,

Bernie

Sam the Postman

Come sit by the fire and I'll tell you another border story.

Forty years ago or so, things were bad around here and there wasn't much traffic across me. Not so much freedom of movement, as the young ones today would say. And there was hatred and prejudice, and many's the one who wouldn't cross over me, one way or the other.

Winnie's da was a fierce man for the politics and he didn't much like the other side. So he wouldn't cross me one way or another. But Winnie herself, she was a wild one, and she loved a dance, and no border would stop her when the desire to jive was upon her. And dance she did, here, there and everywhere, both sides of the border and beyond.

Winnie's da would scold her rightly, but she'd throw up the head and go off to the dances, and say her breezy hellos to me as she passed me by. Well, then, at one of the dances didn't she meet young Sam the postman, and a fair-looking man he was at that time, and is still today, if more wrinkly and less haired than once he was.

But Sam the postman, he was, you might say, from the other side, and when Winnie's da heard that Winnie'd been gallivanting with the enemy, he was not a happy da, so he wasn't. Winnie was a hard one to keep in, but nevertheless he tried, and a misery was felt by all in that house. I well remember the night Sam the postman stood on this bridge here and said to me, 'Border, what's to be done? I'm in love with Winnie and she with me, but the da's a holy terror.'

'He is that,' says I, 'but Sam, you're a postman, with a wee house beside the post office and a fair line in postage stamps. And then, Winnie's da is no border-crosser. You have to use what you have to make your way in life, for love will triumph over hatred.' So we hatched a plan. It went like this: Winnie announced to the da that her heart was broke but she knew the da was right and that she was going to give up on Sam and emigrate to Amerikay for to seek her fortune, or some such ballady nonsense. And the da thought, well, better that Winnie goes off to live her life on the far side of the ocean than that she shacks up with the Sam postman man on the other side of the border.

So Winnie's da took Winnie off to the airport and they said their tearful goodbyes and Winnie flew to New York. When she arrived there didn't she have a cup of tea in JFK and get the next flight back, and was collected by Sam at the very same airport where she'd waved goodbye to the da.

And happily married they were and lived by the post

office. Winnie, to keep up the fiction, wrote the da letters. She laced those letters with stories of the fine upstanding churchiness of the Pennsylvania region, of the savedness of her soul and the many prayers she said. Sam would steam American stamps off of stray letters and glue them on to Winnie's and then deliver them across the border to Winnie's da early in the morning when he'd be asleep. In this way Winnie's da was persuaded that his daughter was living a holy and unsullied life Stateside.

Winnie's da's letters went to an address in Philadelphia. Sam's uncle, resident at said address, forwarded them, so they re-crossed the briny ocean to Winnie and Sam. When Winnie wanted to see her da, Sam would drive her to the airport and she'd fly to New York and then get the next flight back. And there at the airport would be Winnie's da in the Arrivals hall, waiting to see her emerge from those Arrivals doors, all ready and tearful to welcome her back in to the bosom of the home from thousands of miles away even though she was less than ten miles distant most of the year. To get back to Sam, Winnie would be taken by the da to the airport, who'd give her the ticket he'd bought for her, and would wave her off through airport security, on to the flight to JFK, where she would duly get the next flight back to Dublin and be picked up by Sam.

All of which is how come I saw Sam early that morning as he went to deliver Winnie's birthday card to Winnie's da, with its lovely American stamp on it and 'Happy Birthday from Philly' inside.

The promise of peace is like the soft flowing of ice cream out of the big silver machine as it swirls, slowly and deliciously, into the cone of the reconciliation, has the flake of devolution thrust into it and the economic regeneration of raspberry syrup drizzled on to it.

Currently in a taxi with very obnoxious driver who voted for Brexit. Actually there are three other people trying to drive the taxi too and they're all shouting at each other about directions and trying to grab the steering wheel. I didn't even order a taxi.

Stalemate, Jim

In the morning sun, Jim is glistening with frost. He looks almost cute. Almost.

'Morning, Border.'

'Jim. Still here. In the same spot.'

'Aye, but I'm ...'

'... Leaving, I know. You mentioned it. Game of chess later?'

'Maybe, but I could have Left by then.'

'Ok, Jim.'

And so the winter day, which is short enough in itself, passes quite slowly for Jim, mainly because of the now obvious fact that, in Leaving, he is actually going nowhere.

'Right, Border, game of chess.'

'You've set up the board, I see.'

'I have and I'm ready to play. I'm white, Border, so it's me to move first.'

Several hours pass as Jim considers his first move.

'Jim, maybe I should be white.'

'Yeah, ok, Border.'

A Border Guidebook

I felt bad for Rupert, continually sent off to Londinium with the curses of a border ringing in his ears. And then, about a week later, Jean comes by and says, 'Hey, Border, I see your mate Rupert was on the TV thing.' It turned out it wasn't proper television. For a minute I thought Rupert was on *I'm a Brexit Negotiator, Get Me Out of Here*, or *What's My Red Line?* But it was just ParliamentTV – Jean says it's like a soap opera for people who are into politics but don't care about whether there's a plot or anything. Jean says her wee dog watches it with its head over to one side and then falls over, asleep.

Rupert was appearing in front of the House of Commons Committee on Exiting the EU. He had a smile on his face but you could see by his eyes that he was crying inside. The chairwoman said to him, 'Mr Robbins, thank you for attending today.' She mustn't have known he prefers Rupert. 'Perhaps you could begin by updating us on your negotiations with the Irish Border.'

Rupert was pulling a wee bit on the collar of his

shirt. It's probably warm enough in those admin buildings. 'As you'll know,' he said, 'it is often noted that the border is frustrating Brexit. I can confirm that negotiating with the border is genuinely quite frustrating.'

You'd have to feel for him really. He's only a civil servant. He has no more notion of what Brexit is than his boss does. Or the people who voted for it. How can you expect them to be any good at it when none of them have done it before? Still, they shouldn't swagger around the place like they know what they're at. Remember when you were at school and some kid boasted about how brilliant they were at yo-yos, or Tomb Raider, or Scalextric or something like that, and you were a bit intimidated, and you went to their house, and you saw them play it and then you realised they were completely useless at it? That's Brexiters and Brexit. So there was Rupert, being given a going-over in front of a Select Committee looking into something that is impossible and that none of them understand, expecting Rupert to talk about it as if he'd got it all under control and as if they all knew what the actual f*** they were at.

And when it comes to me, well, these head-the-balls are something else. 'The border, Mr Rupert, it's easily solved. We all know it's ...' and off they go, spoofing like the Mayor of Spoof City on Annual Spoof Day. They remind me of Saturday nights round here when all the drunk oul fellas stagger out of the pubs and spout guff about things they're gonna do to sort whatever it is they have on their hammered brains: 'Oh aye, mate, no fuckin' probs, like, you lave it til me, I'm the boy for that,' they say, before they trip over a bin and spill curry sauce on their best shirt.

I thought to myself, what Rupert needs is a guide book to the Irish Border. Then he can keep it under his desk, like a kind of cogsheet when he's next in front of the Committee.

So I wrote Rupert a book ...

The Irish Border

A Brexiter's Manual

This is Prince Brexit. He has a shiny suit of armour and unbounded self-belief derived from his days at an expensive boarding school. He believes he can slay the Irish Border dragon and release Brexit from its captivity. He read on Twitter that the Irish Border is easily solved.

What a looper.

This is the Irish Border. Also it is the British border in Ireland. It is squiggly. It is divisive. It's been there for a while and, to be honest, no one really likes it. Which is a bit unfair because it's actually quite nice. Anyway, it's a peaceful place this last twenty years, SO WHY ARE YOU MESSING AROUND WITH IT?

This guidebook explains what could happen to the border in Ireland, or @BorderIrish, if Brexit actually happens.

This is an ordinary border family a few years in the future. Little Sinéad has spotted a hedgehog in the garden. 'Look, Daddy,' says Sinéad, 'a wee hedgehog. Can we keep it as a pet, please, Daddy, please?' Daddy says the hedgehog hasn't been properly inspected for Sanitary and Phytosanitary purposes. Plus it has no number plates and everyone knows animals crossing the border now need number plates, appropriate insurance and evidence that they are authorised to cross the border once per year as part of the Hedgehog Quota Agreement. 'But what shall we do, Daddy?' asks Sinéad. Daddy is already on the phone and soon the men come and arrest the hedgehog. Sinéad learns a lesson about the stupidity of post-Brexit borders.

This is Seanie. (It's pronounced 'shawny'.) He was a proper farmer before Brexit. Because of Brexit he has had to sell his herd of cattle and his flock of sheep. It was too difficult to move milk across the border and the sheep absolutely refused to go to Larne for export because they said, 'Larne's an absolute sh*thole, so it is, Seanie. I mean, what sheep with any self-respect would want to be exported via Larne?' Now Seanie farms avocados and keeps herds of Americanos.

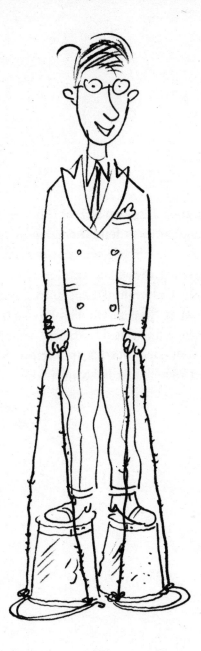

This is Sebastian. He is an MP and he strongly believes in Leave. He also likes feudalism, dressing up, horses, killing foxes with a pack of tongue-lolling dogs, cake and port. Sebastian is an intellectual, he says. He cherishes the Union and therefore wants Northern Ireland to stay as part of the UK as long as he doesn't have to go there himself. Here he is coming up with a solution to the Irish Border problem. He remembers this trick with the buckets from his nanny and thinks it might help goods lorries straddle the border.

Sebastian is explaining to his wife and children how the Irish Border came about because of the ingratitude of the Irish and how it naturally fell into place to protect the Unionists in Ulster who think they are even more British than Sebastian and his family. 'Really, Daddy, they think that?' says Tom. 'Yes, Tom,' says Sebastian. They are all silent.

Sebastian's wife is considering her options.

This is the Irish government preparing for Brexit. The Taoiseach is saying that they should prepare for Brexit as best they can. The Minister for Foreign Affairs is saying this is like when your da has a mid-life crisis and goes to test-drive a sports car and he can't fit into it and you all tell him not to buy it but every dinnertime he goes on about the f***ing sports car and the more you laugh at him the more determined he is to get it. And they all agree.

Sebastian's wife has taken the children to live at their house in France because she can't take any more. 'You can't leave,' said Sebastian. 'No, you can't Leave,' they all said together. Now Sebastian's wife has a successful career as a social entrepreneur. She also gets to eat excellent bread and cheese every day. Sebastian is still an MP, but he is a little worried about his majority.

Five years later Sebastian and his friend, who is Brexit personified, are worshipping big stones. They would love some nice cheese but they are too proud to admit it to each other.

This is the Irish Border after a stupid Brexit. Everything is clogged up. It is not seamless. It is not frictionless. It is very seamed and very frictional. What a disaster.

Bernie McFadden & Co

Solicitors, so we are

Newry and Border Area Branch

7.1.19

Dear Border,
Happy New Year, like.

Jean says you wanted to no about No Deal. Ah
Holy Jesus, it'll be shocking. You would never
have seen the like of it. Big pile of sh~~ite~~, so
it will be. Like the time McArthur's slurry
spreader emptied on you and you sued him. But
sure it might never happen.

Cheers now,
Bernie

Interview

The Irish Border: 'I'd like to look like Tilda Swinton but I'm worried I'm going to look like the 1970s.'

Born in 1921, the Irish Border has divided the island of Ireland ever since. It has helped define the post-Independence Irish state and Northern Ireland. After the signing of the Good Friday Agreement it went into semi-retirement, but has recently taken on a starring role in the unlikely hit comedy *Brexit Means Brexit*. It also has a Twitter account.

What kind of accent do you have?
Sarcastic.

Best friend?
Jean. The US–Canada Border is quite cool, but a bit intimidating. The Good Friday Agreement is on Twitter too, though obviously it's younger than me and it says things I don't understand.

What school did you go to?
An elite bordering school. I don't want to talk about it.

Who is your secret crush?
Definitely the Øresund
Bridge. It is also a tunnel and
it's a border between
Denmark and Sweden. It's
the sexiest border in the
world. I've tried everything
to get it to notice me. I even
tapped up the Swedish
Ambassador to the UK
when she got in touch with
me on Twitter, but no dice
so far. I'll keep trying.
Unrequited love is painful,
though.

**What side of the border
do you get out of in the
morning?**
I don't have sides. I'm a
line, and a line doesn't have
sides. A line is just a line.
I have things on either side
of me – like cows and grass
and dandelions and nice
people and not so nice
people and politically
different states. But I don't
have any sides myself.
Actually, I don't have a
bed either. Or a body to put
in a bed.

**What's your favourite
sport?**
Tennis. I love the line calls.

Least favourite sport?
Cricket. It's like Brexit – long,
tedious, incomprehensible
and invented by the English.
And it turns out they're crap
at it.

**Who's your favourite
comedian?**
David Davis was good when
he used to do that thing
where he sat in the chair
and just talked any old
rubbish that came into his
head.

Favourite TV show?
Line of Duty.

**Least favourite TV
show?**
Brexit's Got Talent, but at
least it's short.

What do you do to relax?

I listen to Mozart and I read a lot. I have developed an unusually expansive and capacious vocabulary which exceeds that normally required for a border to carry out its everyday duties, but I have found this an extremely efficacious facility to possess on Twitter because it makes me look intelligent, especially when compared to Brexiters, who don't.

What's your view on a united Ireland?

They should play 3-5-2, use wing-backs and try not to be so defensively minded.

What do people most misunderstand about you?

I'm the Irish Border, but that makes people think I'm Irish in a passporty, diddly-aye, *Riverdance* and U2 kind of way. But I'm just a border on the island of Ireland. Some people think I'm the Ulster Border, or the Northern Irish Border, or a UK border. To be honest, people are a bit thick sometimes, especially about borders. What can you do?

Who would play you in a movie?

Andrew Scott could do a good me, but just in the Moriarty voice. Tilda Swinton would be great at playing me if it was an art-house movie with swaying grass and dark clouds and a slightly surreal plot. In my own mind I'm very Tilda Swinton.

When were you living your best life?

The eighteen years after the Good Friday Agreement up to Brexit were glorious. Peaceful. I was able to fade into invisibility, but also to exist at the same time. I divided the island and held it together and nobody even noticed I was doing it. It was a great time – all peace, harmony and ice cream. And then Brexit came along and I had to get back on duty. Now I'm on Twitter most of the day being sarcastic about Brexit to try to annoy it.

What would you like to look like after Brexit?

I'd like to look like Tilda Swinton but I'm worried I'm going to look like a dalek.

Is it tiring being invisible at over 300 crossing points?

I'm invisible all over, and no it's not tiring. It does mean that people talk about you as if you're not actually there. That's quite annoying. That's why I'm on Twitter, I suppose. To make myself heard. It's galling hearing people talk about you as if they understand you, and think you're a problem that can be solved by technology when they can't even work a smartphone.

Who owns the fish in Lough Foyle?

Oh, the fish. I have no idea who owns the fish. Why are Brexiters obsessed with fish? I think maybe it's because fish swim around with their mouths open and have a very short memory. I really dislike sea water and I can't swim. I refuse to go in the sea. I have also no idea where I'm meant to be in Lough Foyle or in Carlingford Lough so I just guess, if I'm ever forced to go in the water, for official fishing rights purposes, but generally I stay out of the sea and nobody seems bothered.

Who is your favourite Brexit commentator?

I like the new Brexit Party because their tone of voice just gets a wee bit higher every day as they become more outraged and Brexit moves further off into the distance. They make Jean's wee dog howl. And I love the people on Twitter who tell me to retire, or get harder, or get in the sea – they're all so cute.

What do you prefer: the Good Friday Agreement or the Belfast Agreement?

I call it Good Friday Agreement because we're friends and that's what it calls itself. It's gone all double-barrelled recently: Good Friday-Belfast. It loves that on-the-one-hand but then on-the-other, be kind to all living creatures, ah now none of that arguing, kind of thing. I call it Good Friday because you can get the train from Newry to Belfast, but you can't get it from Newry to Good Friday.

Do you have an Irish passport?

I don't need a passport. I just bilocate around the world and appear in a grassy disguise. If you follow me on Twitter you'll see that I've been to London and Dublin and even to Chequers once and my disguise is impenetrable.

Was Northern Ireland getting boring?

God no. I *am* boring. I like being boring. The alternative to me being boring was a bit drastic, to be honest. It wasn't 'a bit less boring', it was the complete opposite of boring. I like being boring. I'd like to go on being boring.

- Jean, what's the difference between *the* Customs Union and *a* customs union?
- Think of it like the difference between a lovely big bowl of raspberry ripple and a wee small cone of vanilla that somebody has licked, dropped on the floor, and then handed to you with cat hairs on it.
- And what about No Deal?
- Dandelion-flavoured ice cream.
- Does that even exist?
- It will if there's No Deal.

WTF, Jim?

Norway. Obviously I'm sceptical of the Norway route to Brexit nirvana, but I thought maybe, in the spirit of cooperation, I should see if it might provide Jim with a little bit of momentum.

'When you Leave, Jim ...'

'... which will be soon, Border ...'

'... which will, for sure, be soon, do you favour the Norway model?'

'No way, Border. Having Left means Having Left. We can rely on the WTF.'

'Do you mean the WTO?

'No, I'm pretty sure it's WTF.'

'Ok, Jim.'

International Treaties League –
Premier Division

	P	W	L	D	Pts
Good Friday	3	3	0	0	9
Versailles	3	1	1	1	4
Rome	3	1	1	1	4
Withdrawal Agreement	3	0	3	0	0

The Ballad of No Hope, Brexit

I sat around the campfire that night with Leave. Mismatched companions we were, but the trail had brought us together, and as the embers burned and the desert stars shone overhead, Leave told me of its plans for just uppin' and gettin' out of here, travelling to an upland state where the sun shines, the cattle herd themselves and whiskey flows in streams through golden valleys.

'You're a-squatting on yer spurs, Brexit. And yer forgettin' yer international obligations, so to say.'

'And what obligations would those be, Border?' says Leave, aggressive-like and spitting tabaccy juice in the sand.

'I'll tell you a story, Leave, to pass the time, and maybe learn you a thing or two about international agreements and what happens when folk do neglect them.'

And tell him a story I did:

In a sawdust-and-spit saloon in the town of No Hope, Brexit, the wooden half-doors swing slowly open. The wind blows in sand and two weather-beaten cowpokes. The customers look up from their poker and bourbon, and eyeball the strangers like colts that have been spooked. Something about these newcomers just ain't right.

The piano player stops, mid-bar, of an off-key rendition of 'Rule Britannia', and then picks up where he left off.

The acned slopboy rests his rag down on the bar. He wipes his hands on his apron, sidles up behind the grizzled bartender and mutters in his ear: 'Who are those guys?'

The bartender mumbles out the side of a painfully twisted mouth. 'Strand 2 and Strand 3 of the Good Friday Agreement, kid. And if you know what's good for you, you'll pretend they're not here.'

The undertaker nudges the elderly town sheriff. Handlebar moustache a-drooping asymmetrically, the sheriff hitches up his pants and touches his gun belt nervously.

'You two strangers lookin' for trouble? No Hope's a sleepy Brexity town, and I intend on keeping it that way.'

The sheriff's tarnished badge is moving in time to the heaving in his chest. He knows he's seen these gringos somewhere before – maybe on a ranch, or in a bar, or on a poster – but he can't place them. Their expressionless faces are eating into his soul.

A grisly ol' customer slouched over the bar lifts up his head and looks at the dusty silence between the sheriff and the newcomers. 'Them's borderfolk, Sheriff. Ain't no use threatenin' them. They's got their ways of doing things and they ain't much good at listening.'

The strangers turn together towards the bar, leaving the sheriff looking at dust clouds where they'd been. A voice, deep and worn, comes from one of them, though no one in that saloon can tell which stranger speaks. 'Set 'em up there, barkeep. Crossing borders sure is thirsty work. You have what a man might call an aggressive stance there, Sheriff, and it seems a mite out of place. Take a seat. Stop yer gun hand from its twitching. We has the strangest of tales to tell, if the good folks of No Hope has the patience to be listening to it.'

Quiet. Then the sound of the sole of a boot scuffing softly on the dusty floor. Another quietness. The border strangers raise their right hands in synchrony, tip back their hats and stare at their own blue, blue eyes reflected in the mirror behind the bar.

'Some of you folks sure have short memories.' The sheriff's a-scratching at his beard as if recall might be asleep in there. The undertaker's finger runs like a springing mule around the inside of his shirt collar.

'Me and my brother, we were forged in this here town,' the stranger continues, like a coyote calling back across the valley. 'Out of this town and its hinterlands, out of its dust and its enmities, me and my brother here were made, and like worn horseshoes we've been cast away.'

The barback whispers to the bartender, 'Is this the Lord's truth, pa? These strangers, they sprang from the red earth of No Hope, Brexit?'

The first stranger looks the boy straight in the eyes and says, 'Back then, kid, it wasn't No Hope, and Brexit was a foolish man's dream.'

The bartender puts his hand on the boy's shoulder. 'Son, them was different days. We believed in lost things. Soft things. Good Friday things. Ain't that so, Sheriff?'

But the sheriff doesn't answer. He's staring at the stools where the strangers had been sitting. The sheriff, the undertaker, the drunk, the bartender, they're pale and sweating. Across from the two empty chairs, there in the mirror, the strangers' reflections linger on. But the strangers are gone. 'What is it, pa?' says the barback. 'What you gazing at? You're scaring me, pa.'

Bernie McFadden & Co
Solicitors, so we are

Newry and Border Area Branch

22.1.19

Bout ye Border,
Aye, you could seek to amend a motion but you'd
really be wanting a Bill
that became an Act of Parliament to get the
job done.

But here, listen til me, I could take the boat
to London as your representative, and then run
in, pick up the big mace, swing it o'er my head
and shout 'I don't recognise the legitimacy of
this Parliament'. I've always wanted to do
that. It won't help but it'd be some geg.

Cheers now,

Bernie

Rate Your THE IRISH BORDER Experience

The Irish Border ☺☺☺☺☺ 11,861 Reviews

☺☺☺☺☺ 24 February 2019

Michel B
EU

Très belle

Oh, c'est magnifique. The people, the landscape, the humour, and also the strategic importance in terms of maintaining the hard won peace, not to mention the Twitter … More

The Irish Border ☺☺☺☺☺ 11,861 Reviews

☺☺☺☺☺ 15 February 2019

Jacob RM
Somerset

Not a problem

I have not actually visited the border in question but one has read about it in one's library and frankly it is a problem manufactured by the European Union to keep us … More

The Irish Border ⊙⊙⊙⊙⊙ 11,861 Reviews

⊙○○○○ 18 February 2019

Ha ha bally awful border

Bojo da Clown
**Islington/
Camden**

Well I really do not see why anyone would want
to visit. There's neither an olive nor a decent wine
to be found in the restaurants and they are an
incomprehensible people … More

The Irish Border ⊙⊙⊙⊙⊙ 11,861 Reviews

⊙⊙⊙⊙○ 13 July 2019

Quite good, probably

Jeremy
Islington

We enjoyed our visit to the Irish Border, though
we will wait until we have a vote at conference
to decide whether we actually enjoyed it or
experienced a moment of false consciousness
… More

The Irish Border ⊙⊙⊙⊙⊙ 11,861 Reviews

⊙○○○○ 15 March 2019

Worth a visit

R. Emain
Islington

We'd never thought about the Border until
recently and then we saw it was threatened by
Brexit so we give it a visit. It's terribly important
that the Good Friday Agreement stops Brexit.
Couldn't understand the locals though … More

Poor Jim

Jean and I would sometimes forget about Jim. He kind of blended in with the background.

'I see Jim's still here, Border.'

'He's been particularly static today, Jean.'

'I'm Leaving.'

'We know, Jim.'

'Woof.'

'Jean.'

'Yes, Border?'

'Your wee dog is peeing on Jim's leg.'

'Woof woof.'

'I'm Leaving.'

Now, at this point on my Twitter version of this endless dialogue with Jim, some of my followers expressed their sympathy with Jim. That's understandable. He's an unfortunate character in many ways. In the hope of lifting his spirits a little, I told him that there was a groundswell of empathy out there for him.

'Well, Border, your followers are forgetting that I'm Leaving because I staged an idiotically simple referendum on a complex issue, dog-whistled my way through it while trying to avoid the outright expression of racism, and now I'm standing here, politically paralysed, because I'm clueless as to what to do next, so I'm blaming everyone else.'

'Ok, Jim.'

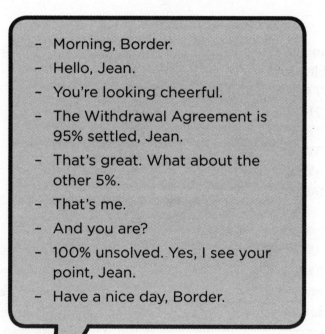

- Morning, Border.
- Hello, Jean.
- You're looking cheerful.
- The Withdrawal Agreement is 95% settled, Jean.
- That's great. What about the other 5%.
- That's me.
- And you are?
- 100% unsolved. Yes, I see your point, Jean.
- Have a nice day, Border.

Spotter's Guide to Brexit Fauna

The next time Rupert came to see me he seemed a bit distracted.

'You look a bit preoccupied, Rupert.'

'I am.'

'And you're standing in Northern Ireland.'

'I am.'

'In the preoccupied six counties.'

'Sorry?'

'Doesn't matter. What has you anxious?'

'Animals, Border. I'm worried about animals.'

Now, this was a bit of a coincidence. The day before I'd had a visit from an EU delegation along with a **very important** member of the Irish government. I don't want to say who it was – confidentiality – but let's call him Simon. After the EU lads had stood around for a while in their Italian suits and looked serious and pointed at stuff for the cameras (do you ever notice politicians can't stand anywhere near me without pointing at stuff?) and had made sure they hadn't got any sheep shit on their shoes, they went off to Dublin for some proper food, but Simon lingered behind. 'I want a word,

Border,' says he. 'Well, fair enough,' I said, 'I could hardly deny you that and it's not as if I'm busy with something else.' So off we went down to the quiet end of a field and talked for half an hour. I was unsettled by what he said, I don't mind telling you, but you have to keep a good face on you when you're at these diplomatic ventures. As we wandered back up to his limo we chatted about the GAA and our favourite desserts but my heart wasn't in it. Then he shook hands with Jean, and drove off.

Jean looked at me, and the wee dog turned her head in a quizzical fashion. 'You're looking a bit pale, Border,' said Jean.

'I'm beyond the pale, Jean,' says I. 'I think I'm going to faint.'

'Bad news?'

'Have you heard of SPS, Jean.'

'Are they a delivery firm?'

'No, it's sanitary and phytosanitary inspections, Jean. SPS.'

'Woof?'

'You may well ask, wee dog. Cover the wee dog's ears there, Jean, and I'll tell you.' So Jean put the headphones on the wee dog and while she was swaying gently to the sound of Mozart's Clarinet Concerto in A major, played by the Academy of St Martin in the Fields, conducted by Sir Neville Marriner, I explained to Jean about phytosanitary inspections just as Simon had explained it to me.

'Given the importance of agriculture to our local economy, Jean ...'

'Oh God, yes, Border. Every other person round here is a farm animal.'

'True. Given that, any change to the regulations on agricultural exports would be devastating for trade in this region.'

'There's all the post-Good Friday Agreement chickens to consider ...'

'You're distracting me, Jean. Simon was pointing out to me that amongst the EU regulations on agri-products are the sanitary and phytosanitary rules, which he has now taught me to shorten to SPS, because if you use an acronym it sounds like you know what you're talking about. So here it is: if you bring a pig across a border into the EU, someone has to have a wee chat with the pig. Or cow. Or goat. Or sheep. Or chicken. This also applies to turkeys, partridges, guinea fowl and possibly even pheasants but we didn't discuss them.'

'To check their ... credentials?'

'Jean, you have to put a glove on that goes right up to your elbow and then use some lubricant and then check their ... credentials. You have to find out if they have any diseases or suchlike.'

'That's a nasty job, Border.'

'It is that,' I said. 'But there's no other way to check except to do it first-hand, as it were. Added to which, Jean, I am not in possession of any arms or indeed any hands, being but a conceptual geopolitical line of largely historical importance.'

'That'll be a disadvantage, even with the benefit of a glove.'

'I told Simon that, but he says there's the four freedoms of the Single Market to protect, plus the fifth freedom. "What's the fifth freedom, Simon?" I asked, and he says, "It's the freedom that means that, whenever the EU tells you to, you have to stick your arm up a cow's ..."'

'Another reason why there can never be a hard border, Border.'

'I am not poking around the insides of farm animals under any circumstances, Jean.'

'No.'

'Nor am I going to be sniffing at chickens to see if they're chlorinated. Nor asking dogs for their passports, present company included.'

'We need to stop this, Border.'

'Woof. Woof. Woof.'

'Did the wee dog hear us, Jean?'

'No, she's listening to the Third Movement, Rondo: Allegro. She loves this bit.'

So, as I was saying, coincidence. Animals were on my mind too. Rupert similarly was agitated by animal welfare, agri-foods and particularly by milk products. I was generally agitated by arm-length gloves and the prospect of ice cream shortages due to problems with the dairy processing supply chain. Now that I think about it, Brexit is obsessed with animals. Here's a wee guide to some Brexit animals:

 **Chickens** – 'Why did the Brexit chicken cross the road?' 'I don't know, but it smelt like a swimming pool', was the joke everyone was telling. Well, I was anyway. Chlorinated chicken is a big controversy in Brexit because the Americans dip their chicken in chlorine to kill off the large corporate farming disease they rear it in. It doesn't work, of course. You can still catch neoliberalism off an American chicken. In Europe we just catch late capitalism off ours.

 **Cows** – I love cows. Cows are going to kill Brexit altogether. Something like 100 million gallons of cows' milk flows from one side of me to the other every day, following the paths of little milk rivers that have existed since the time of Cúchulainn. I might be exaggerating a bit, but there's a lot of milk crosses me and it's a hard thing to put a barcode on it because it's a liquid, obviously. The cows won't stand for this nonsense, you wait and see.

Foxes – there's a Brexit lad called Liam Fox and he really gets on my nerves. I know Tories like pointlessly chasing foxes, but this Fox has a reputation for pointlessly chasing trade deals. Oscar Wilde said Liam Fox is 'the unpalatable in pursuit of the unfeasible' and I agree with that.

Unicorns – Brexit pursues unicorns, so they say. Mythical creatures with magical powers funded by mysterious donors, unicorns hold the secret to wisdom, happiness and eternal life. They can't sort out Brexit, though. If you ask them if they know how to make Brexit work they just say 'Neigh' and a cloud of glitter comes out of their toothy mouths. Useless animals.

Weasels – weasels own the entire parlance of Brexit. When you think you have a word to describe Brexit, it turns out the weasels already own it, and that the word means the opposite of what you thought.

On the way to see me Rupert'd been stopped in the road by Brendan, the oul cattle farmer. Brendan's a grand lad, but over the years he and his cows have taken on very similar characteristics. Brendan has a big long head on him and big, bulgy eyes and sticky-up ears. And you'd recognise him coming by the, let's say, shared cattley odour. Brendan had asked Rupert to stand in a gap while he brought in the herd and I'd imagine Rupert wouldn't see the like in Islington, or wherever it is he hangs his hat of an evening. 'Those are lovely-looking cows,' Rupert had said to Brendan. Rupert would himself not be overly familiar with the bovines in general and was just trying to make polite conversation. The last cow he saw had two kids in it in a Hampstead Heath school play, but you can't fault him for effort with the locals.

'I believe you're correct about animals being central to the problems of Brexit, Border,' Rupert said to me, all melancholy.

'I've never known an ideological version of populism which was so obsessed with animals of all genera and variety,' says me. 'You know there's a rumour, Rupert, that dogs will need passports to get across me after Brexit once I'm a fully fledged EU border with a third country? You're going to have some explaining to do with Jean's wee dog next time you see it. And then there's Seanie's dog.'

'I don't know Seanie, but I do hope his dog hasn't been inconvenienced by Brexit.'

'Well, it has, Rupert. Seanie's severely inconvenienced,

never mind the dog.' And I told Rupert about Seanie and his dog.

Seanie had been passing me by the other day and had paused on the way over me.

'Seanie,' I said.

'Morning, Border.'

'New dog, Seanie?'

'Woof.'

'Hello, Seanie's big dog. That's a grand dog. A dog in need of much walking by the looks of the fine legs he has. Does the big dog have any talents?'

'Oh aye,' says Seanie. 'See this stick?' And he picks up a stick that was just sitting there on the ground and he fecks it away. Whoosh it goes, spinning down the field with the big dog after it. 'Now, wait 'til you see, he won't bring it back 'til I call his name. Fuckbrexit! Fuckbrexit!! ... Ah, c'mon. C'mon, Fuckbrexit!! Bring the fucking stick, Fuckbrexit.'

'He's just sitting there, Sean. He followed the stick, I'll give him that. But he seems a little reluctant to pick it up and return it to his master. Does this happen a lot?'

'It does, Border. When you say his name he's meant to come running to you, but instead he just sits down and looks around him and goes nowhere.'

'That's awkward. And not just for the stick trick. People do say Fuckbrexit a lot round here.'

'You're not wrong there, Border. It took me and Fuckbrexit two hours to get down Hill Street the other day. I mean, we met Mrs O'Connor and she said, "Ah Seanie howareye and how's yer ma?" Then she starts talking about the weather and then she says, completely out of nowhere, "I was just thinking to myself there, Seanie, Fuckbrexit." And so the big dog sits down. You can imagine yourself, sure every other person I meet when I'm out walking the mutt says "Fuckbrexit" at some point in the conversation. If it wasn't that they'd all been saying it for two years now I'd think they were having me on.'

'That makes walking him a bit of a chore, right enough, Sean. Have you had the dog long?'

'No, sure I bought him off a fella in the pub.'

'And was he always called Fuckbrexit?'

'No. That's the thing. I changed his name because I thought the old one would be trouble.'

'What was he called?'

'Fuckingstormontdonttalktomeaboutstormont.'

Sometimes Rupert looks like he wants to shout 'Fuckbrexit' himself.

I invited a delegation from the unions of various border farm animals to meet Rupert as the representative of Her Majesty's Government. I hadn't told him. In hindsight, I should have forewarned him. It was all a bit Dr Dolittle, but with added *Animal Farm*. I did the translation.

'Rupert, this is the representative of the Monaghan and District Bovine Workers Union.'

'There's no one here except you and me, Border.'

'There's a cow.'

'But no union official.'

'There's a cow.'

'The cow is a union official?'

'Who else would be the union official for cows, other than a cow, Rupert?'

'This is ridiculous.'

'Moo.'

'Morning, cow. I know, but give him a second chance.'

'Moo?'

'Well, in my opinion, cow, it's likely to affect nearly everything. What do you think, Rupert?'

'You're taking the piss, Border. This is the second time today someone here has tried to persuade me they can understand cows and it's not even elevenses yet.'

'Moo?'

'I know, cow. I think it's a stupid idea too and I agree that the consequences for cross-border agri-foods are serious.'

'Moo? Moo!'

'Yes, indeed. Ireland is already regarded as a single phytosanitary unit for agricultural purposes, particularly in the case of infectious diseases. But, as I was telling Jean earlier, this might change.'

'Moo!'

'No, I'm not saying, cow, you're ... you know ... infectious. But you might be one day.'

'Moo. Though, moo?'

'That's a tricky one.'

'Because moo.'

'Look, I don't know, cow. Maybe Rupert can explain.'

'Moo!'

'Are you finished talking to cows, Border? Is it possible we could get back to the substance of our negotiations?'

'Baa!'

'Sheep! How's things?'

'You can't be serious, Border.'

'Baa. Baa?'

'I'm not doing so good, sheep. Worried about the Brexit. But thanks for asking.'

'Baa. And baa. And then baa.'

'Yes, I suppose that's true.'

'Ok, Border, fine. What are the sheep saying? Something about grass, I suppose?'

The sheep gave him some stare, so they did.

'No, they were just saying that they think Brexit is a global manifestation of the abuse of amorphous populist traits in neoliberal capitalism being played out at a local level and that we shouldn't assume that the politics we've known is an explanation of the politics to come.'

'Perhaps we should ...'

'Call it a day there, Rupert?'

'Yes, please, Border.'

And off he went.

'You've a bit of dung on your shoes, there, Rupert,' I called after him.

Dear Sir,

I write to assure your readers, even the ones who are not preservers of the precious Union, that my government is very clear that there must be no going back to the border of the past. The border of the future must not be the border of the past, even though I'm very clear that the future will be different to the past and the present isn't worth looking too hard at. I'm very clear.

Yours,

THERESA MAY, MP,
Prime Minister of the Precious United Kingdom of
Northern Ireland with the rest of Great Britain
(caretaker)

Dear Sir,

A recent 'letter' in your 'newspaper' from the 'Prime Minister' suggested that she is very clear on the Union. Not as clear as we are. The border, the thing which defines our very existence as Unionists, must not become a political issue. It's a red line drawn by a red hand on the red bank balance that would be Northern Ireland's financial situation unless it was subvented by the UK government. The EU better wise up. That's all we're saying. Nothing more.

Yours in the Union,
DUP

Cher Monsieur,

We write to respond to the letters in your newspaper from Prime Minister May and the DUP. *Vraiment*, we don't really know what to say. How do you put up with these people? They come to Brussels, eat the confectioneries, drink the good coffee, shout at us, and go back on Ryanair complaining about the lack of free peanuts. How can we be expected to negotiate with that? But at least they do not stay long with us. You have to live with them. We will be in Ireland soon to see the border. It is, at least, a little *drôle*.

With best wishes,
The EU

How's it going there, local newspaper,

Who'd have thought the border itself could write you a letter and get it published, hey? Hello, Jean! I'm in the paper! Thanks for the loan of the iPad. Ah here, local newspaper, this is desperate, though, isn't it? What's the way out of this? I think they should just feck the ring into the mountain and then we could all go back to normal.

Take it easy now,

THE IRISH BORDER
PS: Do you pay people for these letters?

JIM!!!!

One of those lovely quiet days on the border. The birds are singing, but not too loudly. The traffic is passing over me, but not too heavily. The clouds are clouding but not too cloudily. Meanwhile, in Westminster, they're all shouting at each other.

'BORDER!!!!'

'Jim, you scared me. What's the problem?'

'You know how I'm Leaving?'

'Yes, Jim.'

'Well, I'm beginning to think ...'

'Think what, Jim?'

'... that arguing with myself all day about it isn't helping.'

'Well, I find it very entertaining, if that's any comfort, Jim.'

'Thanks, Border.'

Norway

Now, Norway is a nice place, apparently. It has a lovely border with the EU. Too much physical infrastructure and too many checks for my liking, but grand all the same in its own post-Viking way. Brexiters sometimes gulder at me, when I'm patiently explaining the difficulties posed by Brexit in terms of goods, customs, services and the Peace Process:

'Norway!'

That's it. They just shout 'Norway!'

Then it turns out that when Brexiters talk about Norway all they mean is that there is somewhere in Europe that is not in the EU and isn't weird. Norway is, on the whole, I say, taking everything into account, a bit socialist. They also have a heap of oil, which means they can afford to be socialists. Anyway, Norway is not in the Customs Union – 'Woo hoo!' says the Brexiter. But it accepts the rules of the Single Market including freedom of movement. 'Booooo!' says the Brexiter. This is where Norway+ comes in for the Brexiters. The '+' in Norway+ really means 'because we can't think of anything better'.

I suggested to Brexit that, if it thought maybe Norway+ would work, it should go to live with Norway for a trial period. Just to see how it liked being Norway. And it did.

But it didn't tell Norway it was coming. Norway texted me:

> Brexit is here. Did you send it? It says it wants to 'kip on the couch while it gets its life together'. What does this mean?

> Brexit is a bad house guest. It used all the milk and now it wants to know why there's none in the fridge.

> I asked Brexit to do its own washing but it can't because it's watching the football. I think this Norway+ will not work.

I thought we were friends, Irish. Why did you send this Brexit to me? It is rude and lazy and pretends it has gone for job interviews but it just drinks my beer and complains about the food.

It is singing Dam Busters song. You must come now.

Brexit chooses Norway like it's hitting the shops on the last day of the sales when the shop's about to shut and it just *has* to buy something and it grabs Norway+ off the rails thinking, I'll look cool and suave in this, and gets home and realises it looks like an absolute plank and anyway Norway+ doesn't fit and the shop's sale policy is no refunds on sale items and there it is stuck wearing Norway+ for its spring attire when everyone else looks gorgeous in their Canada+s and WTOs but Brexit looks like a fake Viking who's lost in Milton Keynes and its credit card bill is seriously overdue.

Norway every time a British politician mentions it:

- Well, Jean.
- Hello, Border.
- Woof.
- Ah, wee dog, how are you?
- Woof ****ing woof ****ing Brexit woof ****ing Parliament ****ing ****ers.
- Do you want me to translate for you, Border?
- No, it's ok, Jean, I think I got it.

Borders Anonymous

I was feeling a bit over-Brexited. People would be talking to me, but all I could think about was having a wee look at Brexit. I'd be reading a novel, but my attention would wander and I'd realise I was yearning for a dose of Brexit. I had Brexit on my mind all the time and if there was no Brexit around I got jittery and anxious. I had become dependent on Brexit. I was mainlining Brexit. Jean said there had to be a support group for that kind of thing. Yeah, I said, it's called Twitter. 'No,' said Jean, 'everyone on Twitter is a Brexit addict too. What I mean is a group of your peers. People – well, not people, exactly – who can support you through difficult times. I'm your friend, Border, and I love you dearly and everything but I'm not ...'

'... an international border under attack from an amorphously stupid new form of right-wing politics that doesn't know what to do with itself?'

'True,' said Jean. 'But I was going to say I'm not qualified to deal with — with an addict, Border. Plus you're an awful pain in the arse these days and I'd really like a break from listening to you.'

'You're right,' I said, just to keep her happy. But I knew what this meant. And I didn't like it. I had to go to Borders Anonymous.

They meet in a basement. I can't tell you where, but let's say it's east of here and has an air of dark secrets, morbid deeds and enclosed misery about it. Quite old-style bordery. I stood – well, hung around – outside for a while. A few borders went in, mostly in disguise. Finally, I thought to myself, I have to do this. I need to do this. I will do this. I am going to do this. Plus, Jean will kill me if I go back and try to spoof my way out of it. So I went in.

The room was dark around the edges but I could make out a poster with advice on it for coping with Facebook addiction and one warning that putting pictures of your dinner on Instagram is bad for your health. There were the borders, sitting around in a circle. Some of them were fidgety, some of them with the long stare on them, some of them looking fit to fight a continent. I knew most of them from Bordering School. All the bullies and show-offs, all the swaggery, smart-arse borders. All here to unburden their borderi-ness on each other. It was like being back in the dorms, and I hated it. I had just turned around to leave when the Chair Border (and wouldn't you know it was the Swiss–German Border, pompous eejit) pipes up in his wee squeaky proper voice, with the fake sincerity in it:

'Good afternoon everyone. It looks like we have a new member of the group today. Everyone say hello to the new member.'

'Oh jolly japes, Swiss Border, for we know it is of course the British border in Ireland. It is super-duper British, just like me. Isn't that right, British border in Ireland? Fish and chips and mushy peas, eh? Let's play polo after this, I have a spiffing horse.'

'I prefer to be known as the Irish Border these days, Gibraltar,' says me.

'Haha, you have become native, British border in Ireland! I thank the Lord this has not happened to me. No, despite being in the Mediterranean, I still am just like the Homer Counties in England, playing with the crickets and drinking the warm bears.'

'Jesus H ...'

'Please sit down everyone. And let's make the circle of borders a proper circle. Now, new member, perhaps you would like to introduce yourself.'

'How's it going, lads,' says I.

'Oh. No, no, new member. At Borders Anonymous, we must introduce ourselves formally to the group so that we can hold each other on the journey to healing. And we must begin by saying, with honesty, what our issue is. Let's see. Lesotho, why don't you show our new friend how it's done.'

'Hello, group. I'm Lesotho and I'm completely surrounded by another country and it's claustrophobic. Oh my God, I hate it – I mean, I can't breathe. I can't get any privacy. It's like ...'

'Thank you, Lesotho, that's enough. So, you see, friend, how it is done. You must introduce yourself and confess to the group your border problem, and we will be here for you, providing you with a safe environment in which to unburden yourself of your geopolitical problems. Won't we, group?'

Now, to be honest, there wasn't much of an enthusiastic response to this, but Swiss Border seemed to think it was hunky-dory, so off I went.

'Hello, my name's the Irish Border ...'

'We know that, for fu—'

'... and I am addicted to Brexit.'

Some of them sat up a bit. I thought to myself, I need to get some respect here. So I lathered it on a bit.

'I'm completely addicted, like. I eat, sleep and sh*t Brexit. I'm never more than 280 characters away from Brexit. If I have no Brexit for even a few minutes I start to hallucinate. I imagine eating physical infrastructure and ... [building up to the clincher here ... you probably know what's coming ...] ... inspecting chickens.'

There was a gasp. It was a low blow, mentioning the chickens, but I thought to myself, well, it's the God's honest truth, and they might as well hear it. Anyway they're an awful bunch of tossers that used to bully me at school, so they can listen up and be impressed with me for once.

Swiss Border took a while to gather itself, but, to be fair to it, it's very professional. 'Well, Irish Border, it is a difficult journey you are on but I am sure we can all relate to your experience.'

144

'I can't.'

'Korea, please, that's not very supportive. We hold each other in Borders Anonymous.'

'I'm just saying, I can't relate to the Irish Border. I mean, I love physical structure ALL OVER ME. But I wouldn't think about eating it. This new border's a weirdo.'

'That's really not very helpful. We all have issues.'

'Not freaky let's-eat-checkpoints fetishes. Not, feed-me-metadata-about-a-referendum-until-I-can't-function-anymore issues. That's just oddball behaviour.'

'Actually, I take it back. I agree with you, Korea,' said Switzerland. The bastard. It was meant to be the Chair Border or whatever, the leader of this supportive network. 'I mean, we all know you have the big, macho stand-off thing going on, Korea, but still, you're basically right. Irish Border, you are indeed behaving strangely.'

'I haven't even started to tell you about the backstop,' says I. 'Then I'll be like a para-border, a border you can see and not see, a border that's here, there and everywhere. There'll be bits of me in different countries, miles away from myself. I'll be taken apart and scattered to Liverpool and Stranraer and Dublin. There could even be a bit of me in Larne. You borders think you have grim places along your lines. But none of you have anything as soul-sappingly apocalyptically tenebrous as Larne. And you make light of my addiction to Brexit? If a part of any of yous was being repositioned under the leaden, moonless skies of Larne Harbour you'd be worried about it too.'

Switzerland's dander was up now. 'Speaking as the epitome of a European border ...'

'You're such a snob.'

'What?'

'Nothing.'

'Hmm. Speaking as the epitome of a European border, I think you should look at the interfaces around my cantons as a cure for your problems.'

'They won't work,' I said. 'There's too much waiting around at you and too many of those things that look like you're going to order a McDonald's from your car.'

Then the weirdest thing happened. A voice, disembodied, sounding like the shattering of glass, as if from years away and yet, somehow, here at the same time, said, 'Have you considered reunification?'

'Who said that?'

'They say this room is haunted by the ghost of the post-war German Border,' said Norway, in its gloomy, fatalistic voice.

'I felt a chill there. Did you feel a chill?'

'I definitely felt a chill.'

'Lads, listen. Can anyone here offer me any advice on how to wean myself off Brexit?'

'Dude,' piped up US–Mexico, 'you take my advice. Stay strong, believe in yourself, leave yourself open, and we will prevail. We will overcome, man.'

I nearly cried. 'Thank you ... dude,' I said. 'Dude' didn't sound right coming from me. It sounded like the past tense of 'do'. But US–Mexico appreciated the gesture. We were about to high-five when this wee voice muscles in.

'I'm very British, you know.'

'You're not, Gibraltar.'

'I am. 100% utterly British, old bean. Arsenals and Tripping Up the Colour and so on.'

'You live in the Mediterranean, mate. You're Spanish.'

'Now, group, we must respect Gibraltar's self-image if we're to help it on its journey to full self-realisation.'

'It's an idiot.'

'Mushy peas!' blurted Gib.

'Order, borders,' said Switzerland. 'I call this meeting to close. Let's say together our twelve-step prayer.'

I didn't know it, so I listened while they all intoned together:

Divine Line,
We pray that we may be divisions which bring
healing.

Divine Line,
Where there is discord, let us clearly demarcate it.
Where there is grass, let us be fences.
Where there is water, let us not get into unnecessary
disputes over fishing rights.

Divine Line,
Blessed are the humans, for they have allowed
themselves to be defined by us ...

I slipped out. In the woods around the building the birds were singing, the sun was passing its rays through the trees like those stick things in Kerplunk, and all was cool with the world. And yet I thought I could smell the salty, oily tang of Larne Harbour, even though it was hundreds of miles away.

'Well, how did it go?'

'I really felt healed, Jean, you know?'

'And how's the Brexit Twitter addiction?'

'It's funny, Jean, I've hardly looked at it since I got back from the group session, and even then it was only to check out a hilarious video of a cat helping a duck to get across the road.'

'That's great, Border. You seem more yourself already. Goodnight, then.'

'Goodnight, Jean. Goodnight, wee dog.'

'Woof.'

Off they went. And I spent the next three hours reading Twitter threads about the World Trade Organization.

Njim

Jim would have you in a panic some days. Hard to tell the difference between him and someone who's, you know, not entirely with us anymore.

'Jim. Jim. Jim!'

Jim has this rigid kind of smile on his face. Maybe not a smile. Maybe more of a grimace. Or a gurn. Yes, a gurn.

'Are you ok, Jim?'

'Ahm neavin.'

His face isn't actually moving in any way as he's talking. It's quite impressive that he can make these noises. Still, I've no idea what his intended meaning is.

'Sorry?'

'Aaaahmmm NEAVING.'

'Oh, you're Leaving, is that it?'

'Mmmmm.'

'Ok. Why are you talking like that, Jim?'

'Ahm aralysed, Order. Omletely nable ta move.'

'Paralysed?'

'Nnnn Yes. Ut Ahm neavin.'

'That's great, Jim.'

RADIOBORDER

192.1FM

Today at 5pm:

- **How do they get the ripple in?**
- **What's a backstop when it's at home?**
- **'Catch Yerself on There' – Jean's advice column**

The Badger

There's a lad, well, more an aul fella, round here named The Badger, on account of his beard and hair, I suppose. One night last year near Christmas he stood on the bridge that goes over me in Belcoo and he looked down at the running water.

There's many the one around here who is tough on the outside but soft on the inside, and when that softness comes out they like to confide in me. Maybe it's the anonymity of my being invisible, or just my reassuring nature.

'Border,' Badger said to me, 'when I look into these churning waters I see things – Christmases gone by. You remember them yourself. Wasn't there a terrible darkness back then, Border? Thirty years ago. Awful darknesses.'

And then he smiles to himself. 'Still and all, there was some glee to be had. Do you recall wee Seamie? He'd some mouth on him. Long gone now he is, and silent. I dream of him, Border. Don't be telling anybody now, they'll think I'm soft. I can see his face in the waters here this night, Border. There was the time

Seamie told his ma he'd get the turkey, you recall? Seamie's ma was a fierce one. She'd skelp your arse as soon as look at you. Seamie rolled out with a few drinks on him late on that Christmas Eve and says he to me, "Badger! Here, Badger, listen – I've no f***ing turkey."

'Now, I'd had a few too, Border, and I don't mind admitting it. Says I, "Well, Seamie, you're fucked now, mate." "Holy God, Badger," he says. We stood right here on this bridge, Border, and we contemplated. "Except," says I, "Seamie, when you think about it, what's a turkey but a big chicken?"

"Well, there's truth in that, Badger," says Seamie, "but it's shag all use to me."

"Oh now, Seamie," says I, "aren't you and I standing here at the border, and what is it we are looking at?"

"A river," says Seamie. "Is it a trick question?"

"And?"

"The border?"

"And. Beyond that?"

"And McNulty's chicken farm."

"Aye," says I. "And a chicken is, Seamie?"

"A disappointing turkey, Badger."

"True for you," says me, "and the very solution to your woes." So me and Seamie, we weaved across you, Border, all stealthy like, to McNulty's, and we eased open the wire fence, which was open a wee bit anyway. Now McNulty, as you've probably heard tell yourself, Border, was known as a lazy farmer. He'd dump a load a feed for the chucks afore he headed to the bed on a Saturday night, to have the lie-in on a Sunday. So them chucks, being full of seed and weighed down, were easy to catch. And despite the undeniable fact that we caught the biggest chicken in McNulty's filthy shed, and despite the fact that we did the deed, and stripped that chicken to its very essentials, as you might say, well, there was no denying that it was grand chicken but, in truth, a disappointing turkey.

"Maybe it's the drink in me making me melancholy," says Seamie, "but Badger, it seems to me doubtful that the ma is going to be persuaded that this here's a Christmas feast."

"I'm with you there, Seamie," I says. "There's no doubt that a woman of your ma's insight and perspicacity is unlikely to be persuaded, even with a fair wind, good will and a dim light, that this is a turkey as generally understood, and especially so at the festive season. Nevertheless, Seamie, being in possession of a disappointing turkey is better than being in possession of no class of turkey whatsoever."

'So we carried that wee hen, swinging there all naked like something seen through an unpulled curtain, into McNulty's yard, and we stared at it in the Christmas moonlight.

"I'm still fucked, amn't I?" says Seamie.

"Have faith, Seamie," I says to him. "Have faith."

'McNulty was a poor farmer, but you'll remember yourself, Border, he was a great man for the tractors. And he had a fair line in air compressors for the tractor tyres.

"Seamie," I says, "tie up one end of that chuck." And

he did. And, with the hissing and squirming end of the big air compressor, we pumped that chicken full of the best high-pressure air in all of Fermanagh. Seamie bound up the other end and the two of us bounced the big inflated chicken all the way back to Seamie's house.

'At the door, swaying with emotion and probably a bit of the drink too, Seamie says to me, "Badger, you're some f***ing man." And I says, "Happy Christmas, Seamie," and we parted. Now of course the next day Seamie's ma cooked the big inflated chicken for four hours plus and the f***ing thing came out of the oven like a charcoal partridge. Didn't she bate the crap out of Seamie with a wooden spoon and put his Christmas present in the fire?

'That was a proper Christmas, Border. Goodnight to you,' says the Badger. And off he went.

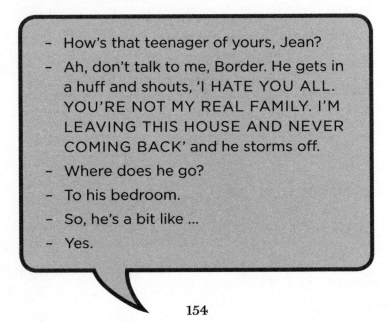

- How's that teenager of yours, Jean?
- Ah, don't talk to me, Border. He gets in a huff and shouts, 'I HATE YOU ALL. YOU'RE NOT MY REAL FAMILY. I'M LEAVING THIS HOUSE AND NEVER COMING BACK' and he storms off.
- Where does he go?
- To his bedroom.
- So, he's a bit like ...
- Yes.

Sorry, Jim?

As you know by now, Jim, for all his arse-about-face and largely ineffectual attempts to actually Leave, is a mild-mannered kind of Leaver. But every now and again his frustration gets the better of him.

'This is all your fault, Border.'

'What is, Jim?'

'All of it.'

'You deciding to Leave, Jim?'

'All except that.'

'You not knowing how to Leave?'

'Ok, not that.'

'You saying we'd agreed on how you were Leaving and then coming back and saying we actually hadn't when you realised what it was you'd actually agreed to?'

'Ok, maybe not that, but all the rest.'

'Jim, sometimes I think you Brexiters live in a sound-proof room so you can't hear the rest of the world.'

'Other people all over the world live in soundproof rooms and you don't hear them complaining.'

The Irish JRM

'Are you Jacob Rees-Mogg?'

'Yeeees. And you are?'

'The Irish Border. Or the British border in Ireland. Bane of your Brexit. Thwarter of your dreams.'

'Ha ha, Border. You are amusing. You're really not a problem, you know.'

'Arragh, thank ee, thank ee, sir, fer the solving of meself agin. 'Tis lost and awandering I'd be if tweren't fer yerself an yer kindness. God an Mary bless ye an keep ye and may the Brexit divil hisself ne'er lep up out o the fiery depths o hell an bite yer arse, begorrah.'

'I'm sorry, can you translate that into Latin?'

Bernie McFadden & Co
Solicitors, so we are

Newry and Border Area Branch

1.3.19

How's it hanging Border?

I hear you want to sue Brexit. You could do so under the Dunderheads and Clodpates Act of 1703, which allows for sentient geographical features to put public representatives in the stocks. I'll have to check this one, now. Then there's the Don't Thee Be a F██ing Edjit Act of 1432. That's a good one, but it hasn't been used for a while. The miscreant has to offer you an ass from their chattels, so that'll be no bother to Brexit, hey?

Right so,

Bernie

How Did We Do Today?

ME: Hello, is that Customer Support?

CUSTOMER SUPPORT: Hello. This is Border
    Technology Customer Support. Your call is
    important to us.
If your query is about trade tariffs, please press 1 and
    have your credit card ready.
If your query is about the death throes of
    neoliberalism, press 2.
If your query is about transferring to another
    continent, press 3.
For all other queries, please hold.

Thank you for holding. We are trying to connect you to
    one of our Customer Support Technicians.

   [Vivaldi plays]

ME: *[sotto voce]* It's a Nigel Kennedy recording, Jean.
    These people have no class.

[Four Seasons later]

CUSTOMER SUPPORT: Hello, my name is Lars and I'm your Customer Support Technician today. Please note that this call may be recorded for training purposes. How can I help you today?

ME: There's drones over me, Lars.

LARS: I understand that may be difficult for you. May I ask, which border am I talking to?

ME: Irish Border. I might be down on your system as the British Border In Ireland Which Is Merely A Temporary Obstacle On The Road To The Fulfilment Of The Destiny Of The Irish Nation.

LARS: Irish Border. I have you here. You're very crinkly.

ME: Squiggly, Lars. I'm squiggly. Anyway, there's drones over me, Lars. Hundreds of them. They're humming. I never asked for drones.

LARS: I understand. Drone tests are part of the Alternative Arrangement Experiments. Border Technology PLC was mandated to carry out those tests. We sent you the contract.

ME: The contract was a sticky note initialled by the UK Prime Minister, Lars. Nobody from the EU knows anything about this. I rang Michel Barnier. He said the EU never agreed to this.

LARS: We sent you an email.

ME: Yeah, I don't know anything about that, Lars, but these drones have been driving me mad. It's like being covered in moronic bluebottles. There's cowpats round here that have fewer wee buzzy things hovering over them than I do.

LARS: These drones will maintain your seamlessness and frictionlessness into the 5G era, Irish Border. They will even 6G-proof you until fully digital borders arrive after 7G. Or maybe 8G.

ME: Well, this is the thing, Lars, they won't.

LARS: Ah, like your Remainer friends, you sit on the sidelines and snipe at those who propose real solutions.

ME: Snipe is an unfortunate choice of word, Lars, but it's not a million miles from the truth. Shotgun is maybe a more accurate term.

LARS: ... No. You haven't? You've shot our drones?

ME: Not me, obviously, Lars. I wouldn't do that.
    Anyway, I can't, practically speaking. But, you know
    yourself, the farmers round here, they don't much
    like crows. And crows is only handled one way.
    With the old two-barrelled solution.

LARS: How many?

ME: Five hundred we've downed so far, Lars.

LARS: Oh my.

ME: So I was just ringing to check, is that them all?

LARS: Yes, Border. Five hundred.

ME: Right ye are, Lars. Job done. Have a nice day.

    [Vivaldi]

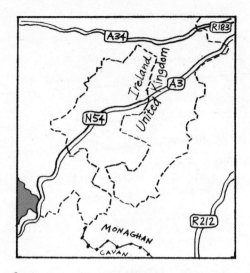

People often say to me, 'Border, how the hell did you end up that shape at Drummully' and I say, 'Ah c'mon now, what's the one thing that would have me so distracted?'

I know I'm a bit of a strange shape. Back when Cúchulainn was chasing cattle over me he was in pursuit one day of the Red Bull of Cúailnge and didn't his bootlace come undone and slip out of his Doc Martens and lie there on the ground, stretching from Lough Foyle to Carlingford, for he was a large-booted individual, and this made the line of the border. It was then submerged for many centuries and only rediscovered by a Victorian antiquarian whose book on the bootlace happened to be on the shelf when Michael Collins and Lloyd George were making me. Borders are funny things, aren't they?

Don't Jump, Jim

'Are you really ready for Leaving, Jim?'

'I am, Border.'

'I worry about you, Jim. How have you prepared yourself for Leaving?'

'By telling you that I'm going to Leave.'

'Yes, and I have, at this stage, definitely got that message. What about behind the scenes, you know? How have your detailed preparations been going?'

'I've mainly just spent my time telling you that I'm Leaving, over and over again.'

'Is that it?'

'I've told myself I'm Leaving too.'

'So that there's no doubt about the fact that you're Leaving?'

'Exactly. It's a managed No-Deal Leaving.'

'It's a cliff edge, Jim.'

'What?!'

'A cliff edge. Leaving without a Deal. It's a cliff-edge Brexit.'

'I'm scared of heights, Border.'

'Oh, sorry, Jim. Well, listen, it's only a wee cliff.'

'Show me.'

'Well, it's like this one.'

'It's quite a long way down, Border. How am I going to manage my No Deal if it means jumping off a cliff?'

'Well, just walk up to it slowly, turn around, place your feet six inches apart, close your eyes, and fall backwards while singing "Jerusalem".'

'Thanks for managing my No Deal, Border.'

'That's ok, Jim.'

- Hello, Border. Do you remember Seamie's parable about the dodo?
- The male dodo that was convinced it was the last dodo and ended it all by jumping off a cliff?
- Aye.
- And at the bottom of its fall it landed on the last female dodo and killed it?
- [Together] ... Brexit.

'CROSS-BORDER?'
'Absolutely livid.'

**What a perpetual downhill
slalom of self-deceiving stupidity
this is.**

You can say what you like, I won't take a fence.

The internet is so slow around here that
I get tweets from the 1930s.

 At least the band on
the Titanic all played
the same tune.

I dislike Brexit but, speaking
as a border, I do admire its
ability to completely divide a
country.

The Withdrawal Agreement

Britain is leaving the EU. Hurrah!

This is what Britain thought leaving the EU would be like.

But it turns out it's not like this.

The bullying EU is making plucky little Britain sign up to the wrong Brexit. Look at the EU's sharp teeth and insistence on the indivisibility of the four freedoms.

There is a Withdrawal Agreement. 'Sign here,' says Monsieur Barnier.

But King ERG of Britain knows this is a trick.

'This is a trick,' says King ERG.

'*Imbécile*,' says Barnier.

Not everyone in Britain likes Brexit.

This is Justin Time. His car factory will be completely buggered by Brexit.

King ERG says Justin Time is a Remoaner.

'Imbecile,' says Justin.

The DUP do not like the Withdrawal Agreement. They think it is the work of Satan.

Here they are, waiting for the PM to make them an offer. They are reading that bit in the Bible about Mammon.

The Withdrawal Agreement includes the backstop. No one in Parliament understands it.

Imagine you are drowning in icy water because some idiot told you skating on it would be ok. Then the EU comes to save you. That's the backstop.

Some people in Parliament are looking at Norway as a solution. Well, Norway but with a plus, because they think just Norway isn't good enough for the UK.

They can see Norway. It is telling them to f*** off.

The Meaningful Vote comes down to three deals in a boat. No Deal, May's Deal, or another vote. None of the deals has a paddle. Or a map. Or a compass. And each one hates the other two.

This is sh*t creek.

The Diary of a Border, Aged 97¼

<u>21 November 2018</u>

Jean's wee dog is sick. Boked everywhere. Rain.

Rupert was here. He says things are at a delicate stage in the negotiations around the Withdrawal Agreement. He says we have to go into 'the tunnel' in order to negotiate a way forward to a deep and special relationship. I'd prefer if we went on a few dates first and maybe met each other's parents but this is the way Rupert does things. I think it's important to tell you, dear diary, that I haven't a f***ing clue what's going on, but apparently I have to go to Brussels because I'm a key stakeholder.

<u>22 November 2018</u>

I'm in the tunnel. It turns out 'the tunnel' is just a way of negotiating without letting the DUP or the ERG know what's going on. It's so boring. Rupert says the Agreement is shaping up but the fish are being difficult. And the cows.

I'm only a border but even I know that where your vets are when they examine your cows is not a very good definition of sovereignty.

Pizza for dinner. No ice cream.

23 November 2018

All the jokes I've suggested putting into the Withdrawal Agreement have been edited out. Still, it's looking good. If a bit long. I said to Rupert, it's like Henry James had written the Good Friday Agreement. Rupert says he's never read Henry James. Or the Good Friday Agreement.

Pizza again. Still no ice cream.

24 November 2018

Rupert's flying around the tunnel like a bee in a flower shop. The Withdrawal Agreement is going to be finished tomorrow, they're all saying. Sometimes they look at me like I was a bad omen or something.

The croissants are class here.

I was flicking through the Withdrawal Agreement and thinking it reminds me of Jim. It's kind of Leaving and Staying at the same time and still not going anywhere.

Pizza. Ice cream craving very intense. They brought mango granita. Wtf. It's like frozen rain.

25 November 2018

OMG I've just got to the bit about the NI backstop — it's incredibly romantic. I'm totally 100% solved.

Other completely solved things are unsolved in comparison to me. If being solved was a crime I'd be banged up for life. Rupert says what was the Northern-Ireland-only backstop is now a UK-wide, end-stopped backstop, backstopped by a NI un-end-stopped backstop. The un-end-stopped backstop was upended then and stuffed into the loose ends of the WA, so that it looks like it's been stopped but it hasn't. Don't tell the DUP, says Rupert. I told him they'd work it out eventually. They're good at sniffing out betrayal.

Rupert has no nails left.

Pizza. More f***ing pizza. I'm going to kill someone if I don't get ice cream.

26 November 2018

I'm particularly proud of the ice cream section of the Withdrawal Agreement. I'd say that was my main contribution, and Rupert says that together we have protected the future of cross-border ice cream production and consumption, and that future generations will thank us for this. Shag the future generations, I said to him. It's my own consumption of Mr Whippy I'm worried about.

Some baldy lad was on the TV saying something like, 'A deal is better than no deal which is better than a bad deal which is not the deal. A Customs Union is worse than The Customs Union unless you believed that no deal is better than a bad deal but now believe that a deal is better than no deal.' Which means it's doomed.

27 November 2018

The wee Brexiters hate the Withdrawal Agreement. I was in that tunnel for nothing. They're all fighting with each other now. I'm worried there'll be a civil war amongst the unicorns, with unicorn families split down the middle and unicorn foals not allowed to talk to their little unicorn friends who were born on the wrong side of the unicorn tracks, all because of unicorn sectarianism. Jean said it's a funny historical irony that I have created a partition in the Conservative Party. I didn't laugh.

28 November 2018

Jim was standing there today like a telegraph pole, reading the Withdrawal Agreement. I asked him if he was at a good bit and he said he was reading the Political Declaration. I told him he'd like that bit because it's like him. It says the UK is ending freedom of movement and there's Jim, who has been free to move and has gone nowhere these past two years.

Gorged on raspberry ripple and 99s.

If I stop reading novels and get rid of all my watercourses I'll be streamless and fictionless.

At Chequers after dinner they play HaventaCluedo.

I'm not squiggly that's a learning curve.

A farmer just spread fertiliser on me in Fermanagh and I AM BUZZING.

I am the elephant in the room of devolutionary forgetfulness.

I'm sick of this. I'm declaring independence.

DO YOU EVER WAKE UP IN THE MORNING AND FEEL LIKE YOU'VE BEEN RUN OVER BY A TRUCK?

If you cut a piece off Brexit does it regenerate?

Brexit Blind Date

Well, Britannia, you've heard all our lovely Post-Brexit Models say why you'll have the sunniest of uplands if you follow their path. Now it's time to choose your Brexit Blind Date.

Will it be Number One?

Hunky Norway, who just loves customs borders but says a pleasure deferred by paperwork is a pleasure properly verified.

Or will you choose Number Two?

Chunky Canada. He may be a big plus plus plus, with very impressive infrastructure, but he has a far, faraway look in his eyes.

Or will it be Number Three?

No Deal. He'll love you once but then cut you down to size with his massive tariffs.

It's time for your indicative vote ...

Wee Dog, Arrested

'Who's texting you, Border?'

'It's Bernie. Jean, your wee dog bit a Brexiter. She's getting the treatment down at the cop shop.'

'She's more or less innocent, though.'

'Will she talk, Jean?'

'I doubt it.'

'Biting Brexiters is a serious offence, Jean.'

'I don't think the wee dog will see it like that, Border.'

'What if she woofs on us, Jean? They'll turn her with

the threat of the dog pound. I mean, she knows all our secrets.'

'Bernie will defend her, Border.'

'Border, any reply from Bernie?'

'Yeah.'

'Well, what's he say?'

'Ehm ... well, he says, more or less, paraphrasing, as it were, that it's an outrage to canine rights that your lovely wee dog has been charged, and he'll be here soon, and he's sure it's all a mistake.'

'That's great.'

'Yes. Yes, it is.'

> Oh fuck. Like between us Jean's wee dog's mad as a fucking squirrel with crushed nuts. I'll have a word with the sergeant when I get to the cop shop. Can you tell the wee dog to say nothing and not to be snarling at the Guards 'til I get to the cells?

'Is that another text from Bernie?'

'Aye.'

'Well?'

'He … ah … he says he expects the charges to be dropped but they're just … you know …'

'What?'

'Paperwork, Jean. They've just got to do a bit of paperwork.'

> Border, just out of the interview room. Here, don't tell Jean, but I think the wee dog's going to grass on the lot of us, the whole 'we defo need a backstop' scam that you cooked up with the Irish govt included. Do you have any leverage on the wee dog?

'I can't believe this is going to trial already, Border. Any word from inside the court?'

'Just got a text from Bernie.'

'Are they being nice to my wee dog? She has big dark eyes, they'll not be able to resist her.'

> FFS Border the wee dog just said it refuses to recognise the authority of the court. If Jean wasn't your friend I'd gladly see this pup put away.

'A verdict?'

'Yes, Jean ... Bernie says your wee dog is completely exonerated.'

A muzzle and an ASBO. The judge is a Brexiter. If I hadn't got him off a speeding ticket a few years back the wee dog'd be in the pound. Best place for it. You owe me one.

The wee dog's doing a speech to the media on the steps of the courthouse. How did you get me involved in this fiasco? 🍺🍺🍺

Jim, Stuffed

The snow is falling and yet people have that warm glow about them that says, 'Christmas oh my lord despite not having all the presents bought or the turkey I feel a vague love for my fellow human beings.' And then there's Jim, standing to attention, staring at the horizon from where he expects Brexit to arrive and find him, like the wise men turning up at the stable. Poor Jim. It's Christmas, after all.

'Looking forward to the Christmas, are you, Jim?'

'I love Christmas, Border.'

'Would that be because it's a festival commemorating the birth of a child who ends up as a refugee from a vicious state which is intent on its own self-preservation? And that, despite this persecution and displacement, that child grows up to become an adult who preaches love and peace, Jim?'

'Ahm, no. I just like getting presents. And the food. I like the food.'

'Turkey?'

'No way! It would only encourage them to join the EU. Goose.'

'Of course. From ...?'

'Canada.'

'Of course, with ...?'

'All the trimmings.'

'Of course, so it will be ...?'

'Canada goose +++.'

'Happy Christmas, Jim.'

'Happy Christmas, Border.'

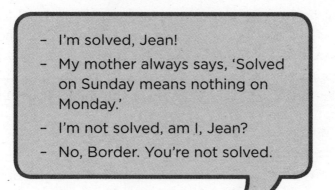

- I'm solved, Jean!
- My mother always says, 'Solved on Sunday means nothing on Monday.'
- I'm not solved, am I, Jean?
- No, Border. You're not solved.

WHAT'S ON TONIGHT

6.00pm

The BorderIrish News

Jean brings us the latest updates on the desperate
shenanigans at Westminster and all that. It'll be even
more depressing than yesterday's news, probably.
Yesterday's news was worse than the day before, d'ye
remember? And still ye'll all watch it. God knows why.

6.29pm

Border Weather

Jean with the latest weather update but I wouldn't
bother because it's going to be raining again.

6.30pm
Whose Line Is It Anyway?
People arguing with each other about who owns the border.

7.00pm
Line of Duty
A revealing interview in which BorderIrish discusses its sense of obligation to the island of Ireland and tries to find out who's the bent copper.

8.00pm
Scandinoir+
British democracy is found murdered, hit over the head from behind with a blunt referendum. Can world-weary DI Irish Border overcome its ice cream addiction, find the murderer and stop this becoming the work of a serial killer? Part 1 of 32.

9.00pm
The BorderIrish News
Same news as at 6pm but wearier.

9.30pm
Fawlty Towers
Xenophobic British man makes an absolute mess of running something.

10.00pm
Midsomer Murders
Documentary about the Conservative Party.

10.30pm
Antiques Roadshow
Documentary about the Conservative Party.

11.00pm
Film: The Wicker Man
People on a small island off the coast of France come up with a weird new religion, go completely mad and burn the whole place down.

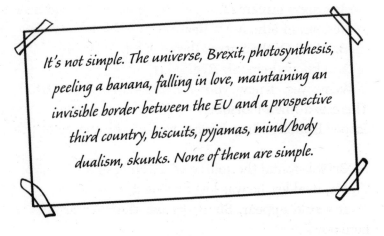

It's not simple. The universe, Brexit, photosynthesis, peeling a banana, falling in love, maintaining an invisible border between the EU and a prospective third country, biscuits, pyjamas, mind/body dualism, skunks. None of them are simple.

Alternative Arrangements:
The Source of Denial

Meanwhile, in the London offices of the Alternative Arrangements Commission:

'Good morning, Sir Reginald.'

'Beakley, how are you? Any post?'

'Nothing, sir.'

'Any appointments?'

'Yes, sir. 10 a.m. A Mr Bribble.'

'Bribble? Of the Sussex Bribbles?'

'You know them, Sir Reginald?'

'Why, yes. Knew young Bribble's father at Eton. There is a line of Bribbles reaching back to the brave Jasper Bribble, who was lost finding the source of the Nile.'

'Bribble found the source of the Nile, sir?'

'No, Beakley, he was lost finding it.'

'It would appear, Sir Reginald, that Mr Bribble is here now.'

'Show the boy in then, there's a good chap.'

Sir Reginald mulled over the appearance of young Bribble. Could be just the chap, he thought. Finding these Alternative Arrangements has been proving damned difficult, don't you know, and it needs a man of Bribble's pedigree, someone with a family history of getting lost and not finding the thing he set out for, to really knock this problem into a cocked hat.

'Ah, Bribble. Sit down.'

'Thank you, Sir Reginald.'

'How's your father, Bribble?'

'He ran off with the cook fifteen years, ago, sir.'

'Yes, of course, I remember now. Terrible business. Fine chef, though. I remember a spectacular coq au vin at your house in the 1970s. Mother well?'

'Dead, sir.'

'Indeed. Well, I'm hoping you're here, Bribble, to help us out with finding a solution to this damnable problem of the Irish Border.'

'I am, sir. Ready, willing and able to assist.'

'Keeping up the family tradition. Excellent, Bribble. Let me brief you on how things stand, Bribble. As you know, we are convinced that Alternative Arrangements to the backstop definitely exist.'

'So you can see, Bribble, we've made a litle progress, but probably not enough. You saw the ad in the *Telegraph*, no doubt?'

'Yes, sir. 500 guineas and an OBE to the chap who can say what the Alternative Arrangements actually are. I'd like the opportunity to give it my best shot, sir.'

'Jolly good, Bribble. Now you're in, I can explain the problem in more detail. We've worked on the parameters of the issue for several days now, and two years ago some fellows in the Foreign Office had a chat about it too. As you know, there must be no physical infrastructure at the border. That now includes buildings of almost all kinds and cameras. Additionally, and this is where it gets really tricky, there must be no customs personnel of any kind, and no military or police to protect them. You can see why, Bribble – given that this is to become an international frontier between the disgusting morass of anti-democratic liberalism that is the European Union and our own glorious nation, home of the mother of all parliaments and Lord's Cricket Ground – we've reached an impasse.' Sir Reginald scratched his head and thought of the comfort of his club bar.

'Sir Reginald, this is where the Bribble acumen gives us, if I may say, a sharp advantage over Paddy and Michel.'

'Who?'

'The Irish and the damned continentals, sir. I have read over the documentation drawn up by our government and the Commission and I believe I have found a loophole, two loopholes in fact, that we can use to our advantage.'

'Oh, Bribble, I knew you wouldn't let the country down in this, our hour of need. You've done it! You've found the Alternative Arrangements! I'll call in Beakley. Beakley! Beakley!'

Beakley is a model civil servant, loyal, patriotic and practical. He is not to be rushed, nor to be easily persuaded. He enters rooms civilly, servantly and civil-servantly, which is to say with polite deliberation.

'Sir.'

'Beakley! Bribble has discovered the Alternative Arrangements.'

'How exciting, sir. Mr Bribble, do please share your discoveries.'

'Not so fast, sir. I have found the path forwards, but not the actual solution.'

'See, Beakley. I told you Bribble would come through.'

'Perhaps Mr Bribble would be so good as to explain.'

'May I use the flipchart?'

'Why, of course.'

'We know that the EU will not allow physical infra-structure on the border.'

'Damn them.'

'I have perused Article 167, Section 3, subsection 4.2 of the Withdrawal Agreement at which one is directed to the definition of a building. It says that any building must conform to the Energy Performance of Buildings Directive (EPBD). In that directive all forms of build-ing material are described.'

'Ye-e-es, and ...'
'But not planks.'

'Not planks?

'They forgot planks. There is no mention of planks in the Directive.'

'The significance of this omission being what, Mr Bribble?'

'The significance being, Mr Beakley – and I resent your tone of scepticism, if I may say so. I find it, frankly, unpatriotic – that planks are not, legally speaking, a "building" in European law, and cannot therefore be "physical infrastructure". If we use planks on the border that will be a perfectly legitimate Alternative Arrangement and the Europeans will have no legal recourse to object. In addition, planks are already in use in several farmers' fields along the border to allow them to traverse farms which straddle said border. Planks may be said, in fact, to be not only inherent to the border's built environment but to be part of its heritage. Planks go back to the ancient Celts.'

'Planks?'

'Yes, planks. Obviously work remains to be done on the way in which the planks are deployed ...'

'Obviously.'

'... but it's legally sound.'

'This is exciting, isn't it, Beakley?'

'Without a doubt, Sir Reginald.'

'Carry on, Bribble. Let's assume the planks work. What about the issue of policing the border? It's an unpleasant place, you know.'

'We have agreed, as you know, that there be no personnel on the border. Here I draw on my ancestor, Jasper Bribble.'

Beakley could not resist. 'The Jasper Bribble who disappeared trying to find the source of the Nile?'

'I'll have you know, Mr Beakley, that Jasper found the source of the Nile.'

'But no one found Jasper.'

'When Jasper Bribble went on his adventure in the Delta, the locals thought his scheme potty. They said it couldn't be done, and they refused to lend him horses or camels.'

'An appalling attitude,' interjected Sir Reginald. 'Really, such people need to believe in the wisdom of the Empire.'

'But Jasper was not put off. Oh no, having tried to find the lost waterfall of Zambia, he had experience of such expeditions. He knew that, better than the horse or camel by far, more loyal and more trustworthy, a greater friend to the adventurer, is the ostrich. And so

Jasper imported two hundred ostriches from Ethiopia to accompany him on his quest to find the source of the Nile.'

'I'm not sure I follow what's happening here.'

'I'm afraid I agree, Bribble. Please extrapolate.'

'Sir Reginald. Mr Beakley. With a combination of these two elements I believe that we can devise an Alternative Arrangement to the Irish Border question.'

'May I interject, Sir Reginald?'

'By all means, Beakley.'

'Mr Bribble. Am I to take it that you are suggesting that, by a combination of planks and ostriches, we can concoct an Alternative Arrangement to the Irish Border problem which will check the movements of goods and agricultural products, provide surety on rules of origin, copperfasten sanitary and phytosanitary inspection procedures, *and* maintain the ongoing arrangements in respect of VAT?'

'I appreciate, Mr Beakley, that the fine details are yet to be teased out, but yes. Planks are very reliable and adaptable. And ostriches show great initiative when given responsibility. They need caps, though.'

'Caps?'

'Jasper's last entry in his diary describes an ostrich rebellion caused by a lack of self-esteem amongst the ostriches. "Must provide caps, if not full uniform" were his last scrawled words. Some say he failed to recognise the stirrings of insurgent ostrich nationalism but I'm certain that giving them caps and possibly epaulettes would have quelled the unrest.'

'Excellent. Well, get to it, young Bribble. This could be the breakthrough we've been waiting for.'

'Sir.'

U OK, Jim?

Jean was surprised to find Jim lying on the ground. Jim had been standing still on one leg since Tuesday to prove that alternative arrangements are possible but he'd just fallen over.

'I haven't fallen over. This is an alternative arrangement to standing,' said Jim.

Jim got up and waved his hanky over his head.

'Are you surrendering, Jim?'

'It's a parachute. It's going to ensure a soft landing.'

'It's definitely a hanky, Jim.'

'You two just don't believe enough.'

'Gravity,' said me to Jean, and Jean to me.

If you can ever see me from space,
we're all f***ed.

Maybe I should go and partition Somerset and see how they f***ing well like it.

There is an invisible Irish border Twitter account which is much funnier than me but obviously you can't see it.

I'm like a crop circle, but interesting.

If you trample on Brexit gripes you can make Brexit whines.

85% of the UK's toilet paper is imported, so let's hope Project Fear doesn't *really* scare people.

Brexit is ridiculousing on the border.

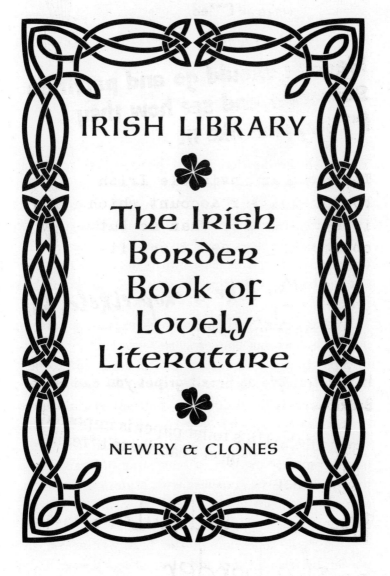

IRISH LIBRARY

✦

The Irish Border Book of Lovely Literature

✦

NEWRY & CLONES

On Border Literature

The Irish Border has been the occasion of much woe-betiding and wailing on the island of Ireland. The very soul of the Irish has been rent in twain by the partition which divides this fair land. This island of saints and scholars, once so happily united under warring provincial leaders and ineffective kings, now lies sundered along a line that bespeaks of the broken heart of a nation.

And yet. And yet. Out of such sadness a terrible beauty is born, as Shakespeare says. The border has inspired the best of our bards and scribblers to new heights of self-indulgent reflection on the general state of things. Hunkered down in their garrets, blootered in their snugs and glazed-eyed in front of their blue screens, the writers of Ireland and, indeed, the world, have serenaded the border, have sung its praises, and have cursed its noxiousness with a glorious imagination that is unsurpassed in any literature of Europe, nay, one might say, of the entire globe.

This little collection of the best writing on the border, by Irish writers and some others who've had a wee go at the literature, is testimony to what a wondrous border it is, for, like it or not, it's our border and it is recognised everywhere as a phenomenon, right enough.

Myles NaG

'The Lake Isle of Tariff-free'

I will arise and go now, and go to Tariff-free,
And a small Cabinet build there, of absolute waffle
   made:
No quotas will I have there, and jam from a money
   tree,
And live alone in a BBC-loud glade.

W.B. Yeats

The snow is general all over the border. It is falling softly on the soft border and, further westwards, softly falling into the dark mutinous waves of the Foyle. The newspapers are wrong, though, because they nearly all support a hard Brexit.

James Joyce

I have spread the border under your feet;

Tread softly because you tread on its current lack of physical infrastructure.

W.B. Yeats

My aunt, as was her wont, in the final days of spring, as the garden gate swung to silently, creating a breeze which caused minuscule ruffles of the hairs on my outstretched hand, produced tray-bakes. I bit into a rocky road and was overwhelmed with childhood memories of bordering, and having set up the Twitter account I began to think that as I tweeted each individual tweet, those tweets, like the beams of sunlight on a border river, or grains of sand drifting through waves of time down the same river, or leaves blown from the ash tree into that stream and then eventually out to sea, were but transient things, mere memories, preserved in pixels and perhaps lodged in some repository of passing, unsolicited and as yet unsifted knowledge, floating there in a mass of other desperate attempts to pin down the meaning of the times we inhabit at this angle of unbelonging, and so my unease showed me a path, much as I had seen paths made by the farmer and the smuggler over the decades, paths which opened up and were then, years later, forgotten, covered over with brambles, and it occurred to me that writing my tweets in the manner of Marcel

Proust would be pleasing to me but that it would be unlikely, or, at least, unforeseen, that a border would write like an overwordy French memoirist and yet that if a border did so, and if anyone reading this actually got to the end of it, they might be further convinced of the border's intelligence and, by implication, that Brexit is a load of crap.

Marcel Proust

This is just to say

I am the
softened
border in
Ireland

that
you were going
to harden
for Brexit

Forgive me
but no
I'm too lovely
and cool
William Carlos Williams

The border's an ineluctable modality of the invisible so it is.

James Joyce

Between my finger and my thumb
A complete lack of physical infrastructure

Seamus Heaney

borderrun, past Armagh and EU, from swerve of shore to bend of lough, brings us by a commodius vicus of recirculation back to Hail-mellow-well-fed Castlederg and Environs.

Sir Tristram de Brexit, violer d'amores, fr'over the snot-green Eire sea says he, had referended up here from Uplands Sunny on this side the scraggy isthmus of Britannia Minor to retwitterate his pencilpointless war. The fall (bbbbbbrrrrrreeeee-exxxxxxiiiiiitttttt!) of a once strait oldrighty to bentydoubly newrighty is retweeted early in bed and later on down through all truth decommissioners, atavisionistas, and FaceTimefascistas. Of the first was he to bare arms and a name: BoJo of Incompetency. His crest an omnipluribus, in vermillions of lies, avec deceits rampantly cambridging

analytically, lions trafalgar squaring, trimmed with
fleur de morelies

James Joyceagain

Theresa's Road Not Taken

> Two roads diverged in a border wood,
> And realising I couldn't take either,
> Indecisive long I stood,
> And looked down one as far as I could
> To where it max fac-ed into the ether;
> I had no idea what to do,
> And that has made all the indifference.

Robert Frost

Brexit Breath

[Curtain]

CENTRE STAGE: a pile of miscellaneous Brexit-
related ideas, all scattered and lying. The sound
of a birth-cry. Pause. An exasperated sigh.
Pause. Another exasperated sigh.

[Curtain]

Samuel Beckett

Yes, the tweeters were right: Brexit was general all over. It was falling hard on the Rees-Mogg and, further westwards, soft Brexitly falling onto the dark, mutinous border, whose soul swooned slowly as it heard the Brexit falling faintly on all the living and the dead.

James Joyceagainagain

Wee, sleekit, cow'rin, tim'rous Brexit
O what a panic's in thy exit
Tha well may start awa sae hasty
Wi bickering brattle!
I will continue tae chase an thwart thee
Wi withering tweetle!

Robert Burns

If you've had a f***ing stupid idea and then found out it doesn't f***ing work, don't be going ahead with it just cos you're too f***ing stubborn to admit you've been a f***ing plank.

Oscar Wilde

I have met them on Brexit Day
Coming with livid faces
From county or town among grey-
Haired Remainer spouses.
I thought before I had done
Of a mocking tweet or a gibe
To please a follower
In my timeline's Twitter club.
Unchanged, unchanged utterly:
A risible polity is born.

W.B. Yeats

Change all the clocks, annoy Peter Bone,
Confuse the DUP by leaving them alone,
@ByDonkeys hired the plane circling overhead,
Scribbling on the sky the message 'Brexit's Dead'.

W.H. Auden

Putting a Brexit from the right pocket of his coat into his mouth, Jim replaced it with a Brexit from the right pocket of his trousers, replacing that Brexit with a Brexit from the left pocket of his trousers, replacing that in turn with a Brexit from the left pocket of his coat. In this way there were always four Brexits in each of Jim's four pockets and one in his mouth, but not quite the same Brexits. And when the desire to Brexit took hold of Jim again, he drew on the right pocket of his coat, certain of not taking the same Brexit as the last time.

Samuel Beckett

Brexit

[Curtain]

[Centre stage – pile of discarded items and rancid prejudices]

VOICE 1 *[Tyrone accent]* Ah Jesus.
VOICE 2 *[Cavan accent]* Look at the state of thon.
VOICE 3 *[Armagh accent]* F'sake, like.
VOICE 4 *[Derry accent]* *Sigh.*

[Curtain]

Samuel Beckett

'Tis a wattle-faced purveyor of lies,
A gall of putridity, a mink's claw,
A counsel of despair in a fair land,
A darkness that shuns the candle of truth.
I fucking hate this Brexit, so I do.

Shakespeare

We are all in the gutter, but some of us are lines of geopolitical demarcation tortured by uncertainty and looking at the stars.

Oscar Wilde

This is the Border, I said. It's a Border.

Jim opened a bottle of beer in a middle-aged way.

Sit down, Border, Jim said. I wasn't sure he meant it.

Yeah, I will, said the Border.

You do that, said Jim.

When Jim went out to the garden for a smoke I said, Jim's amazing, isn't he? He's so interesting. I feel very drunk.

Jim's a prick, said the Border.

Sally Rooney

If I look out over Carlingford Lough I can see the Mourne Mountains. It's well for them. They look nice. They remind me of the time C.S. Lewis offered me the job as the Wardrobe, or when Tolkien asked me if I wanted to be the border of Mordor and sometimes now I wish I'd taken it because it couldn't be any worse than this.

Bernie McFadden & Co

Solicitors, so we are

Newry and Border Area Branch

31.5.19

Ah Jesus, Border, you want to know about
taking the red bus lad to court? Of course you
should. The question of the legal obligation
of a Border to attend a court in one its
adjoining jurisdictions has precedent in
Berlin Wall v U2. But here sure why wouldn't
you go to court and nail that hairy lying
f█████er to the wall?

Good luck now,

Bernie

RADIOBORDER

192.1FM

Today at 5pm:

- **Is Jim just a bit crap at Leaving?**
- **Is an abacus a technological solution? Iain Duncan Smith joins us**
- **'Wise up' – Jean's advice column**

Tech, Jim

Jim says the technological solution depends on having enough rechargeable clipboards. He means iPads, I think.

'Or them wee helicopter things the kids have,' says Jim.

'Drones, Jim?'

'Aye, we could use them,' says Jim.

'How would the drones see the goods inside the lorries, Jim?'

'Tupperware,' says Jim. 'Lorries with big see-through lunch boxes on the back of them. You'd need big white labels for the lids to stop them getting all mixed up. There's nothing worse than having a gigantic Tupperware lunch box on a lorry and getting back to the factory and finding you've actually got some other company's massive lunch box lid and it doesn't fit. And a permanent marker the size of a tree to write your name on the label on the lid. Terry McHugh could do it by lifting the big marker up with his front loader. He's very dexterous with machinery and he has lovely handwriting,' says Jim.

Alternative Arrangements
Anonymous

'Welcome to the A.A. Working Group. We are here to support you in your addiction to technology, in whatever form that may take. We will not judge you, though the number of likes you get may affect where you appear on our algorithms. Now, if you could all put down your phones, iPads and abacuses, we can begin the session. Everyone, deep breath. Now, who would like to speak first?'

'Hello, I'm Owen.'

'Hello, Owen.'

'My name is Owen and I am addicted to Alternative Arrangements. It started with an interest in free trade but when I ended up on TV talking about technology that I didn't understand, I knew it was out of control.'

'Feel the love in the group, Owen. Who's next?'

'I'm Dominic. Alternative Arrangements got so bad for me I forgot about the port of Dover.'

'Oh my God, I forgot about Dover as well. I can so relate to this.'

'Thank you for relating to my relatableness, David. I can relate to you resigning as Brexit minister in outrage at what you negotiated as Brexit minister. Also, I wanted to share that I couldn't bring myself to read the Good Friday Agreement.'

'Dominic, I haven't read it either.'

'Nor me.'

'I don't think anyone here has actually read it, Dom.'

'Well, thank you, Dominic. Anyone else like to share?'

'I'm Marcus.'

'Hello, Marcus.'

'Are you going to talk about fish, Marcus, like last week? And the week before?'

'No, I'm not. I want to say that I *love* Alternative Arrangements. I really love them. I want to Alternatively Arrange the whole f***ing country. LEAVE MEANS LEAVE! Take the whole of society and alternatively arrange it. Conservatively!'

'You're upsetting the group, Marcus.'

'I don't care! Leave Means Leave!'

'LEAVE MEANS LEAVE!! LEAVE MEANS LEAVE!!!'

'GROUP!'

'LEAVE MEANS LEAVE!'

'Group, please ... Thank you. Quiet for a moment. So, who's next?'

'If I maaay, my name is Jacob. I and my family, and particularly pater, whose books no doubt you have read, have been addicted to Alternative Arrangements since the restoration of the monarchy.'

'Ooooooh.'

'In order to understand Alternative Arrangements, one really has to acknowledge that the rot set in with the great Reform Act of 1832. As any historian worth his salt will tell you ...

... 3 hours later ...

'... and that's why one really must understand that Alternative Arrangements are perfectly feasible and only a jolly fool would not see that.'

'Zzzzzzzzz ... Oh, right, yes. Quite so, Jacob, and your point about the engineering of the public sewage system in Victorian Birmingham really is a powerful one. Thank you, Jacob. We have a new member today. Would you like to speak?'

'I'm Theresa. I once listened to someone talk about Alternative Arrangements ...'

'F***ing amateur.'

'... and now I'm very clear that I'd like you all to think I'm addicted to A.A. so that I can pass the Withdrawal Agreement while you're all still thinking about Alternative Arrangements.'

'We must all begin our journey somewhere, Theresa.'

'Michel Barnier loved my Alternative Arrangements.'

'Yes, Owen, you tell us that *every week*.'

'Same time next Thursday, everyone?'

'Wait, wait, I have to tell about ... ah ... my ... what's the thing?'

'Sorry, sit down everyone. Boris wishes to share.'

'Ah, yes, well you see, I ... ah ... yes ... Alternative Arrangements ... such things ... well, they've always been my ... I mean ... of course ... we must believe in Alternative Arrangements because ... I know ... It's ... ah ... it's just like the Second World War, when we jolly well defeated the Huns with Alternative Arrangements, didn't we, or like the Peloponnesian War, or, not the Peloponnesian ... Troy ... it's like Troy. And the horse. The horse made of wood ... pulled up to the ... ah ... thing, and then they ... yes, that's it, the Trojan Horse. We just have to believe in the horse, not the actual Trojan Horse, but our version of it, and the various adumbrations of technological solutions to the ah ... border ... trusted traders and such like. Yes. We can do this. If we are more positive in our atmosphere.'

'He's such an inspiring speaker.'

'Just like Churchill.'

'Our journey towards self-understanding has really taken a great step forwards today. Thank you, Boris. See you all next week.'

'See you then.'

I wouldn't mind a wee go at Alternatively Arranging myself. There are bits of me that are uncomfortably squiggly and if I could alternatively rearrange myself before bed I'd get a much better night's sleep.

The Diary of a Border, Aged 97½

14 January 2019

The Withdrawal Agreement isn't going down well in the House of Commons. They don't like it. They don't like the backstop. It's too complicated. Some of them don't like it because it means they will not have Left enough. Some think they'll have Left too much. They're all blaming the backstop.

15 January 2019

Well, they had the Withdrawal Agreement vote and it lost 432 to 202. The government said it could have been worse and they'll try again. It's like that time I went in for Border of the Century and the Berlin Wall got 600 votes and I got 2 and I thought, that wasn't so bad, and then I realised Jean and Jim had voted for me and even I had voted for the Berlin Wall.

12 February 2019

I have hundreds of crossings but I don't think any of them are the road to Brexit.

16 March 2019

I suggested to Rupert that we could do a technological solution by people tweeting me an emoji of what they're carrying in the van and I could tweet back a thumbs up or a clown face or one of those monkeys with its hands over its eyes, depending on how I was feeling. He says he'll think about it.

17 March 2019

Sometimes I think St Patrick missed a few.

26 March 2019

They're going to have indicative votes. Jean says that every morning for the past two years when she takes the wee dog for a walk, she shuts the garden gate, turns in the general direction of Westminster, raises her right hand and gives them an indicative vote.

1 April 2019

Britain is in a terrible state, though. It's awful to see a country so divided.

10 April 2019

They're running out of time. I think the British will need another extension. Jean says it's like that song 'If I Said You Had A Beautiful Body of Existing Legislation That Was Unlikely To Be Reconfigured And Successfully Supplemented By The End Of April Would You Hold It Against Me?'

11 April 2019

They got another extension to the Withdrawal Agreement. Will I ever be an EU border? I've spent hours on Duolingo learning Czech and I still don't know pokud můžu použít.

3 May 2019

I don't think these people know what they're at. Today was one more day of blindfolded shuffling towards the darkness. The blindfold shufflers who have had their fingers in their ears take them out, say 'but, the future?', and return to their own silence. The blindfolded shufflers are arguing with each other about how to shuffle. The blindfolded shufflers have agreed that being blindfolded is not ideal and so they are shuffling more quickly. The blindfolded shufflers are singing the praise of a bright new dawn. Today the leader of the blindfolded shufflers will pause on the path to the cliffs and update the other blindfolded shufflers on their shuffling. That's what I was thinking today.

7 May 2019

There was a lorry parked on the hard shoulder today and I thought, oh no, it's the beginning of the Brexit-lorry-jam-nightmare-tailback-of-the-future, but it turned out the driver just needed a wee.

7 June 2019

Theresa May has resigned. I'm quite resigned myself. It's like a load of people were watching a Warner Brothers cartoon and they decided to elect a different coyote because they think the last coyote couldn't catch the roadrunner because it didn't believe it could. That's all, folks.

Bye, Jim

Jim wants to know if I'll miss him when he Leaves. Of course I'll miss him.

'Yes, I'll miss you, Jim.'

'What will you miss most about me?'

'Your decisiveness, Jim.'

'Really?'

'Yes, your ability to take action without hesitation.'

'But you'll miss me?'

'Yes.'

'Maybe I shouldn't go if you'll be sad.'

'It'll be ok, Jim.'

'I'm not sure.'

'But why does Brexit always have that empty look in its eyes, Jean?'

'Because inside it knows that the fulfilment of its desire is the opening of a void, and that to stand there, alone, having walked a path which shuns all others, is melancholia distilled.'

'Oh, right. Thanks, Jean.'

Will it Never End?

'Jean!'

'Border.'

'I've worked out how it ends. So,

1. Brexit is in this book.
2. I'm writing the book.
3. The outcome of Brexit is dependent on me.
4. Therefore, Jean ...'

'You can write the ending of Brexit.'

'Well, exactly.'

'You just have to decide on an ending.'

'But first, I have to decide what kind of book Brexit is.'

'Genre-wise, you mean?'

'Yes. But easier said than done. I mean, say Brexit was a swashbuckling novel based on the adventures of a great patriotic naval hero of the British empire from the days of the tall ships and the jolly Jack Tars and that.'

'What would the ending be then?'

'Something like ...'

Admiral Leave lies, wounded, on the deck of his ship. The smoke from a thousand cannons swirls through the rigging. Admiral Leave, held in the strong arms of his faithful bo'sun, knows the world is dimming, his life slipping away like an anchor dropping, fathom by fathom. He stretches out a shaky hand to a handsome young officer in the circle of men around him and says, in a whisper that bespeaks of a dying breath and an inner fortitude, 'Kiss me, Brexit.' But Ensign Brexit petulantly turns his face away, unmoved. And so Admiral Leave goes to join the great flotilla in the clouds, with a look of bewilderment on his face for all eternity.

'That's not bad, Border.'

'I don't know. I'm not sure Brexit is a rambunctious tale of seafaring derring-do. Maybe it's a noir detective novel.'

Her silhouette on the frosted glass said, 'Why, hello, honey' before she did. The door swung open.

'Why, hello, honey,' she purred. 'You must be The Irish Border, P.I.'

'That's what it says on the door, ma'am,' I said. I was trying to play it cool but I hadn't felt this way since Øresund.

'I have a case for you, Border.'

'Take a seat and let me speculate. A lady like you wouldn't be in a dive like this, unless what's bothering you was something you're ashamed of. You don't want anyone respectable to know about your trouble.'

'Well, that's as may be.' I could see I had her attention now. I poured us each a Bushmills and tipped back my hat.

'A dame like you values the rules. Straight down the line. But with curves.' We both blushed and had a sip. 'I'd hazard that your trouble is that someone called a referendum, manipulated the result and now they're creating chaos to see it through, and you want me to stop them...'

'That's some speculation, Border.'

'...and the grifter you're looking for goes by the name of Brexit.'

'How ... how did you know?'

'Because I have that very same Brexit in brace-lets ready to be taken to the joint, locked up in that janitor's closet beside you.'

The door burst open and a gang of New York's finest flooded in.

'Where is he, Border?' said the Captain.

'Janitor's closet.'

They opened the door and out Brexit fell. As he lay on the floor, looking like a racoon that's been thrown out of a racoon speakeasy, the dame aimed a mighty kick at his softest parts.

'Take him away, Captain Barnier,' I said, and poured another round.

'Yeah, alright, though I think you're fantasising a bit, Border. Is Brexit not ... bigger? Really big, now – more like a Shakespearean tragedy?'

'Maybe, Jean. That needs a bit more effort. Ok, here goes.'

ACT V, Scene 4

BORDER:
So, how's about thon backstop, Lizzie?

QUEEN ELIZABETH:
As heaven is high and as hell is low
I vouch to thee a perm'nant backstop.

BORDER:
Promise?

LIZZIE:
An English pledge is as unbreakable
As the iron bands on our salty barks.

BORDER:
That's smashing, so it is.

   [Exit BORDER]

LIZZIE:
Send in Lord Brexit, that vile, venomous
Pathway to drownings in moral quagmires.

[Enter BREXIT]

LORD BREXIT:
Your Highness's highness is higher fair
Than the celestial highness of the spheres,
Your ...

LIZZIE:
Your loathsome fawning maketh the bile rise
In our royal throat, Lord Brexit. We boke.
The border shall have its perm'nant backstop.
You shall have Somerset and all its boars.

BREXIT:
The boars of Somerset are mine, my Queen.
Thou givest me what already I own.

LIZZIE:
It was a Renaissance pun. On boars/bores.
The Border told it to me this forenoon.

BREXIT:
Truly the border is a wisecracker.
My liege, the loathsome backstop will ever
Vassal us to the lordship of the Gauls.

LIZZIE:
What about the Germans?

BREXIT:

I'm not sure there are technically any Germans at
   this point in European history. Someone will tweet
   us to tell us, no doubt, having looked it up on
   Wikipedia. But the Gauls, eugh. Coxcombs and
   foxes all.
Hence I humbly request, O Virgin Queen,
That counsel be taken from our allies
In Ulster, those loyal subjects who call
The backstop Satan's putrid pisspot.

LIZZIE:

Hie thee, Brexit. Thou art a cream fac'd loon.
I lovst the border and will bring it peace.
Thou shalt to the scaffold go for treason.

BREXIT:
But, my Queen ...

LIZZIE:
You're some piece of work, as Hamlet doth say.

   [Exit BREXIT]

LIZZIE:
Our tale is told, our song is sung
Brexit, in death, not life's well hung.

   'The drama is good, Border. But Shakespeare's a bit
off-putting, maybe?'

'Aye, you're right. So, big drama, big emotions, but something more contemporary?'

'What about a bit of, you know ...?'

'Why are you nudging me, Jean?'

'*You know*. Like that book everyone has read but pretends they haven't. The one with the tying up in it.'

'Nope.'

'You do. The one that Fintan O'Toole says is like Brexit. A national version of self-flagellation and sado-masochism, or something, he says.'

'Does Fintan O'Toole say that? The dirty divil. I never thought of him as being like that. *Fifty Shades of Grey*, is that it?'

'Aye.'

'I never read it. I'm not doing the tying-up stuff, no matter what Fintan O'Toole likes.'

'Fintan O'Toole doesn't like it himself, he just says Brexit does.'

'Ok, Jean. I'll try an erotic ending so. Here goes ...

Leave turned in the bed and saw, finally, the sensuous, sunny uplands which it had desired for so long. As if years of yearning had become focused on this one, intense moment of freedom, Leave moved towards Brexit. Leave's desire was burning, burning with an intensity which was painful, as if every nerve-ending were on fire, every sinew strained with a pain that was also pleasure, and yet Leave could not move. Brexit's mouth opened slightly, its eyelids closed a little, its pupils dilated, its sunlit uplands glistened, and again Leave leant towards this pure embodiment of every gratification it had ever sought, every thirst it had ever felt, every fantasy it had ever fantasised about. But still it could not move.

'Come to me. I want you. Now,' whispered Brexit.

'I want you too, Brexit. Oh, how I want you. I've wanted you ever since I thought of you. I want all of you, the absolute No Deal of you. The free trade, the freedom from the shackles of European legislation, the hypocritical morality of the 1950s. I want to jump off the cliff edge of passion with you.'

'Then take me,' Brexit panted.

'I can't,' sobbed Leave. 'I can't. It's like there's some kind of invisible border between us.'

'How's it going there?' said a bordery voice. 'This bed is quare comfy. Oh My God Almighty, the two of you are in the buff. Have yous no shame at all?'

'That's the one, Border.'
'Aye, I think you're right, Jean.'

Bernie McFadden & Co

Solicitors, so we are

Newry and Border Area Branch

10.5.19

Well now, Border,
C'mere to me, thon Brexit seems to be bating
many species of shite out of itself over in
London so I'm guessing you're safe enough for a
few weeks now,
til they remember bout you again. I'm off to
Portugal for tax reasons for a wee while. Text
me there if there's an issue. Watch out for
that Johnson lad. He's the kind I see across
the courtroom gettin away with it cos his da
knows
the judge.

Bernie

Deliver Us from Eejits

I woke up one day there and I heard the bells ringing all along me, and I thought to myself that Brexit had finally passed away and the people were celebrating. But no. It was just Sunday again. Jim was still standing there with that patient look on his face. Rupert was on his mobile talking to his new boss about the World Trade Organization and then finding out he'd been sacked. And Brexit was still here, like bad weather.

I looked at the two of them, and at Jean walking her wee dog, and I thought to myself, you don't have to have lived on the border, or in Northern Ireland, or Ireland, or to be (Northern) Irish, to understand the instability and fear, the sense of betrayal at the unravelling of a previously given guarantee, which Brexit brings to this place. It's a choice not to understand it. You could understand if you opened your mind to it.

You know, a few years ago, before the Brexit thing, I imagined that whoever is in charge of these things would say to me one day, 'Border, you've done a grand job, but we've no longer any need for you. We're letting you go.' And instead of giving me an engraved tankard or a carriage clock they'd tell me they'd applied to the EU for funding for that big f*** off Museum of the Border. There'd be a display of invisible replicas of particularly interesting invisible parts of me. In the Duty-free Museum Shop there'd be wee snowglobes for sale with centuries-long prejudices trapped inside them and sticks of rock with nothing written through them, and I'd slowly dissipate into myself and be memorialised only as a fading shadow, or something glimpsed out the side of your memory's eye.

There's a clear sky, and the mild air hangs sweet as the border people hunker down for rest, knowing that another day has gone by and has held their lives and their loves in place, and their Border, like it or not, has kept their equilibrium safe for the time being and for tomorrow and maybe the tomorrow after that.

As night falls dark on my baroque meanders I wonder whatever happened to statecraft, that mixture of idealism and pragmatism that asserts a viewpoint and implicitly accepts the existence of another. I wonder whether it is an inevitability that good sense will return and rescue me. When I look 'north' from where I lie here in the grass and mountains and sheughs, I see people of all kinds: good, caring, thoughtful, loving people; people who are open to change; and people who aren't. It's a complicated, beautiful place. Try to understand it. It's not so different from where you live yourself, you know. It never has been.

Because underneath all this is a deep sadness. The Good Friday Agreement was a miracle of a kind. A negotiation, a compromise, a realpolitik solution where none seemed possible. All that weight of grief and lost possibility turned slowly to something better. And then ...

Look here, I know I've messed around and joked and acted the eejit in this book and on the Twitter account, and maybe everything will be ok, but this time, this Brexit, feels like when your favourite vase is falling from the table and you're watching it as it gets closer to the floor. Maybe it won't break, or maybe you'll catch it, or maybe it'll brush past your fingers and ...

Imagine a border that is curious about how you're feeling rather than suspicious of where you might be trying to get to.

At the Church of the Border you can come and baptise yourself or your children in the renewing waters of my brooks and streams and loughs, and you can leave happy, knowing that you have reaffirmed your commitment to live in whatever way you please, in peace and love.

After nearly 100 years of being a border the most important thing I've learnt is this: borders are the most cowardly form of human interaction. Opening yourself up to strangers, opening yourself up to the new and the unknown and the unexpected – that's bravery. That's what I've learnt, after 98 or so years. Thank you for reading my book – I have some bordering to do now, but would you say a wee prayer for me, please?

Our father, who art in Cavan, Caledon be thy
*   name;*
thy Killeter come, thy will be Down, in Strabane as
*   it is in Lifford.*
Give us this day our Derry bread and forgive us
*   Dundalk,*
as we forgive those who Dundalk against us,
and lead us not into Brexit but deliver us from eejits.

                                        Amen.

Glossary

Backstop – The backstop is my insurance in case the people who sound like they don't know what they're talking about, but do sound like they're up to something else, are up to something else and don't know what they're talking about. You'd think that if the people who sound like they don't know what they're talking about do know what they're talking about and aren't up to something else, then they wouldn't mind an insurance policy against the possibility of their stupidity or malice.

Borderom – the state of ennui brought on by hearing people talk about the Border and Brexit.

Brexit –

(a) 3D chess played on snakes & ladders board;

(b) lemming family day out;

(c) Dadaist IKEA furniture assembly instructions;

(d) neoliberal origami;

(e) an anti-immigration-inspired stoking of nationalism leading to a political, economic, social, diplomatic, agricultural and ice-creamy act of self-harm but what can you do I tried to explain it.

Extension to Article 50 – outline planning permission to destroy your own house.

Free Trade Agreement – when you agree with your neighbours not to tear down each other's houses.

GATT xxiv – pronounced 'gatwentyfor' when said by spoofers to cover up their spoofery. Haven't a notion what it actually means.

GATT xxv – the one where they get married, move to Tuscany, buy a vineyard and produce a delicious and piquant Chianti.

Indicative Votes – votes which indicate that you don't know what to vote for.

Jean – sane person from down the road there.

Playborder of the Western World – play by J.M. Synge in which a Border pretends on social media that it has killed Brexit by hitting it over the head with a spade and then there's an absolute riot.

Sanitary and Phytosanitary Regulations – Eugh.

Singles Market – what people go on Tinder for.

Ulster –
    (a) province with nine counties in north-east of Ireland;
    (b) [inf] failed attempt at a state;
    (c) says no;
    (d) coat with cape, sleeves and lining and a heightened sense of the importance of the Reformation.

Ulysses – novel by James Joyce about Brexit in which a student who's just back in Dublin after his Erasmus year meets an older Irish fella whose father was an immigrant and works in social media, and in which the real hero is a woman who speaks her mind and celebrates her body.

Unicorn-Riders of the Apocalypse (Four) – indie band formed at Eton College. Their single 'Venture Capitalism in the UK' reached no. 79 in the UK charts in 1985.

Wee Dog, Jean's – small canine belonging to Jean (see above). Generally anti-Brexit but capable of being turned by bribery. Has distinctive woof and inability to perform simple tasks.

Withdrawl – posh, Brexiter accent.

Withdrawl Agreement – when a posh Brexiter says 'yeeeeesss'.

No Deal requests the last waltz

Acknowledgements

Many people have contributed to making me the divisive, confusing, contentious and glorious thing I am today. I owe everything to Michael Collins and Lloyd George – great job, guys. The Boundary Commission were a tremendous help in my early years, steadfastly refusing to do anything useful to redefine me and thus preparing me for the endless, pointless, posturing stasis that is Brexit. Also worthy of mention are the Reformation, the Plantation of Ulster, the Act of Union, the Home Rule movement, the Ulster Solemn League and Covenant, and all the generally intractable ideological positions which led to me being put in place in Ireland and have maintained me here ever since. I couldn't have done it without you all. Thanks so much. Thanks also to the Good Friday Agreement for letting me more or less retire, and bad cess to Brexit for threatening to make me work again.

Jean has been a constant companion and my rock of sense through it all. Her wee dog, less so. Jim has been a pain in my arse for three years now but I've kind of gotten used to him. So, yeah, thanks a lot, Jim. I'm

254

grateful for the support of the Borders Anonymous group, except for Gibraltar. The friendship of the US–Mexico border, and our shared experience of 'hairy-headed dumbass m*****f***ing demagogues', has been a source of great solace. The Øresund Bridge never returned my love, but a shout out to it anyway in plaintive, unrequited hope.

Since I've been on Twitter lots of people have supported my account by indulging the fiction of a talking Border enduring the travails of Brexit. Special thanks to Amanda Abbington, Kay Burley, Sarah Carey, @BelfastAgmt, Bonnie Greer, Tanni Grey-Thompson, Deirdre Heenan, Caitriona McMullan, Yvette Shapiro, Feargal Sharkey, Maria McManus, Maxine Mawhinney, Peter Murtagh, @rockallisland, Angela Rohan, Labi Siffre, the late Bernie Tormé, Ali White, Robert McLiam Wilson and Simon Oak (who recorded my ill-fated but, we thought, quite catchy Eurovision entry). I'm indebted to the brilliance of Kevin McAleer's stand-up routines and John Byrne's art project 'The Border Interpretative Centre' (2000). Aideen McLoughlin and RTÉ's *The Business* kindly gave me my first big break on the wireless. Thanks to the journalists who were game enough to interview the Irish Border, most especially to Freya McClements, who got the exclusive for *The Irish Times*, and also to Rory Carroll (*Guardian*), Méabh Ritchie (BBC Newsbeat), Marie-Louise Muir (BBCNI), Siobhán Geets (*Wiener Zeitung*), Armand Back (*Tageblatt*), Raffaella Menichini (*La Repubblica*), Catherine Lough (mollybloomsaysyes.com),

Julien Marsault (Usbeketrica), Brian Mathuna (Headstuff) and Shauna Corr (Belfast Live). Thanks also to *The New European*.

Brexit is complicated. My Lord, but it's complicated. However, Twitter is great because there are actual people on Twitter who know stuff about Brexit, and they tell you about it for free. I've benefitted enormously from the expertise, kindness and good humour of Peter Foster, Viviane Gravey, Katy Hayward, David Henig, Sarah Kay, Brigid Laffan, Sam Lowe, Anand Menon, Steve Peers, David Phinnemore, Nina Schick and Peter Ungphakorn, amongst many others. All opinions expressed in this book are my own and are therefore correct.

Thanks to my agent Robert Caskie for his friendship and expert guidance, and to Liza DeBlock of CaskieMushens for her help. Thanks also to HarperCollins in Ireland: Eoin McHugh, Tony Purdue, Patricia McVeigh, Jacq Murphy, Ciara Swift and most especially to my brilliant editor Nora Mahony for her good sense, wisdom and patience.

I'd also like to thank Wolfgang Amadeus Mozart.

This book is dedicated to a messer whose life was interrupted by the Troubles. A good man, who made me laugh.

Thanks a million to everyone who follows and reads the account. You're all mad, so you are. It's been fun. We shall overcome, some day.